ETERNAL TIES

Other books by Graham Bernard
The Challenge of Evil
Why You Are Who You Are

ETERNAL TIES
The Reality Behind Relationships

A Conversation with
Richard

Channeled by
Graham Bernard

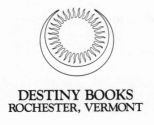

DESTINY BOOKS
ROCHESTER, VERMONT

Destiny Books
One Park Street
Rochester, Vermont 05767

Library of Congress Cataloging-in-Publication Data

Bernard, Graham.
  Eternal ties : the reality behind relationships : a con-
  versation with Richard / channeled by Graham Bernard.
      p.   cm.
  ISBN 0-89281-271-0
    1. Spirit writings.   2. Interpersonal relations—Miscellanea.
I. Richard (Spirit)   II. Title.
BF1301.B4165   1990
133.9'3--dc20   89-78256
                                                            CIP

Printed and bound in the United States

10 9 8 7 6 5 4 3 2 1

Destiny Books is a division of Inner Traditions
International, Ltd.

Contents

IV. Relationships Today

V. Relationships — Unseen

*To Meg, Kathy, and Martha
in gratitude for choosing
to come to us.*

Richard's Preface

It is necessary to understand the purposefulness of your relationships, to see them in historical perspective as a continuing process, to realize that if you live your life intuitively your relationships will be constructive.

Trust your innermost feelings in regard to others. They will lead you to those to whom you already belong. Whether you are the pivotal figure at the center of a large group or whether you are a loner quietly and anonymously reaching out to others, if you follow your heart you will be led to form the relationships you need.

Our own concern in considering this subject is to help people to understand relationships in their essence —potentially divine souls becoming human for the purpose of fulfilling their divinity in relation to one another. Our effort is to make the opportunities and difficulties of life understandable — to help you to understand that your own progress is dependent upon harmonious and constructive relationships. You must grapple with your own divinity. You are to learn through the following discussion who you really are and who others are in relation to you. And most of all you must learn to become a conduit through which God's Love can reach others. This is central to our teaching.

Introduction

Those of you who are familiar with our first book, *Why You Are Who You Are*, are already acquainted with the circumstances of my life that led to its achievement and the subsequent value I feel I gained from the illness and disability that surrounded it.

Since that time there have been more books, and more physical problems intended to remind me of the value of tolerance in our lives as we travel the path toward our ultimate goal. I see in my daily life the need for constant awareness of those elements that can creep in to deter spiritual growth — resentment, doubt, negativism, fear, worry. Seeking harmony in all things is surely the answer. My physical limitations have not deterred me from functioning and making my contribution to Richard's teaching, which is to include six books. I thank God for the privilege.

In this, our third publication and our second in collaboration (I received the material for the first book, *Why You Are Who You Are*, myself, and my wife, Madeleine, and I collaborated on the second and third books, *The Challenge of Evil* and this one), we have discovered important, valuable information concerning relationships as the means through which we grow spiritually. For instance, our relationships did not begin and will not end with this incarnation, and all deterrence in relationships must finally be resolved before we can hope to reach our ultimate goal. We are primarily concerned

1

with love in relationships, and the book is a sober reflection on the value of relationships of blood (family) and relationships of goal (those we love and admire and our close friends with whom we will share our ultimate state) to our purpose in being and becoming.

But once again before we begin to question Richard on the essential value of relationships, it is necessary to restate the Crucial Concepts of his teachings. The concepts contain the essence of this work and therefore warrant your perusal.

CRUCIAL CONCEPTS

1. **Immortality** is a reality.
2. **Reincarnation** is a fact.
3. The nature of **God's Being** is truth.
4. The nature of **God's Will** is construction, which leads to spiritual growth.
5. The nature of **God's Love** is harmony.
6. The nature of **self-will** is deterrence (all that deters spiritual growth).
7. **Deterrent Force** is the collective energy of all thought, action, and emotion that deters spiritual progress.
8. **Constructive Force** is the collective energy of all thought, action, and emotion that contributes to spiritual progress.
9. **Frequency** (the number of vibrations per minute) is the barometer of development. The degree of frequency of all things, incarnate or discarnate, indicates the degree of spiritual growth.
10. The **Place of Self-Deception** is a state of frequency in which those who are unwilling and unable to see themselves clearly remain after death until and

unless they can learn to see themselves as they truly are.

11. The **Place of Preparation** is the state of frequency in which we prepare for our next life. If we can see ourselves clearly, it becomes our "home."

12. The **Lower Regions** are a lower level of frequency in which those who are dedicated to evil find themselves after an incarnation.

13. The **Realms** are the level of frequency in which one finds oneself after one no longer needs to reincarnate. There are seven Realms to be achieved before perfection can be achieved.

14. The **Purposes**, of which there are seven, are elements of the Realms. Each Realm has a purpose that must be gained before one can move on.

15. The **elements of development** are the particular circumstances of an incarnation.

16. Our **spiritual equipment** (love, sense of truth, and intuition) is brought with us to earth from the Place of Preparation to be used to cope with growth problems.

17. **Grace** is the ever-present opportunity to begin again, to start over.

18. The **quality–quantity factor** is basic to the functioning of an incarnation. Quality is earned in the discarnate world, but it cannot become permanent until it is given quantity in the living out of an incarnation in the incarnate world.

19. The **Law of Parallels** is an answering flow of energy from the discarnate world to all thoughts and acts from the incarnate world.

20. **Event** is the culmination of converging circumstances.

21. **Intent** is the plan of a life which has been determined prior to reincarnation.

22. **Deterrents** are deterrent souls in the discarnate world.
23. **Thoughts are things.** Constructive thought contributes to construction as a force at large. Deterrent thought contributes to deterrence as a force at large.
24. **Self-possession** is possession of the temporal self by the eternal self, the ultimate state of humanity.

Before embarking on the body of this discussion, I would like to pause in order to acknowledge the love and industry that Frances McArdle has given in helping to assemble this material.

Richard asked us to think about our relationships and just what they mean to us. This request prompted the question that opens our first chapter.

I. The Essence of Relationships

The Paradox

Since the concept and practice of relationships are undergoing such overwhelming changes, please help us to understand ourselves in relation to others.

Before we start talking about personal relationships let's take time to understand what relationships are. What are we really talking about?

First of all you must understand that it is through relationships that you develop your potential individuality. The paradox is that the more developed your individuality becomes, the more you are part of the Whole. You must realize that you, a unique and independent creation, are a functioning part of the Whole — wholly independent and wholly one with God.

Is this what I am now, or what I should be?

This is what you are in essence. This is your responsibility to become — what you *are* to become.

I can believe we are all unique, but I'm not so sure about independent.

You are in the sense that you have free will.

The Whole could mean different things to different people. How are you using it here?

I mean God in evolution, God as expressed through all of evolving creation. The Whole is comprised of unique, individual creations. We are all part of an interrelated evolutionary process. The evolution of the Whole depends upon and is altered by the evolution of its parts and vice versa.

What exactly do you mean by evolution?

Evolution is that which is — God, that which is, is animate. Animation motivated by purpose develops differentiation. Differentiation through animation results in individuality. Individuality is animation and differentiation fulfilling purpose — evolution.

Would you say then that individuality is the goal of evolution?

For the purpose of fulfilling the Whole, yes. However, that implies the necessity for all individuals to fulfill the potential with which they were created. Any deviation from that effort is deterrent and not one's true self functioning. Because you were created as an individual element of the Whole, you can only achieve perfection by developing in accordance with the Will of the Whole (God), physically, emotionally, and spiritually.

It is well to meditate on this reality. As you think of these things, try to apply each one of them to yourself. Maintaining this kind of awareness will improve your well-being and the way you think about your personal relationships. The entire plan of salvation is based on the fact that you, a unique independent creation, are a functioning part of the Whole.

What is the difference between the One and the individual?

The One (God) became individual with the granting of free will. All diverse individuals are therefore one in essence. Relationships are the means through which

God can function on earth, individualized. Through relationships the individual parts of the Whole become one, and the One becomes individual. Everything else is dependent upon the understanding of this.

Just how do relationships express oneness with the Whole?
By serving as the medium through which love is channeled.

What exactly do you mean when you say that relationships are the means through which God can function on earth individualized?
What you do and say affects your character, and this reflects on your relationships. If what you do and say is constructive this creates harmony within your relationships, bringing God's Love on earth through you. Through constructive harmony within your relationships you emulate God's Will and God's Love and become one with the Whole.

Please define oneness for me.
Oneness refers to the blending of diversity into singleness with a single intention and purpose — a fusion of diverse elements into a complete and perfect Whole. Oneness with the Whole (God) is our ultimate goal, blending our diversity while retaining our individuality.

Please clarify the thought that it is through relationships that we develop our potential individuality.
Through relationships with others you can learn about yourself and, with this knowledge, recognize your relationship to all — your oneness with the Whole.

When God first created the angels, they were discarnate beings who were essentially one with Him — a part of Him. With the granting of free will, those who took that path had the choice of recognizing this fact and acting on it or ignoring it entirely and going their own way, concentrating on self. However, this did not alter the fact of their essential oneness with God. All forms of separation are merely emotional aberrations. The individual remains an essential element of the Whole in potential, whether or not this fact is fulfilled.

Since it is seldom fulfilled, it must take more than relationships to bring it about.
That is the purpose of reincarnation, which is tied to the function of relationships. Reincarnation provides for the survival of the individual through birth and rebirth — the survival of the individual soul in both the seen and the unseen worlds. The individual brings about diversity through relationships, and the diversity becomes one through relationships.

In order to grasp this fully, I need to understand diversity in this sense.
Diversity is an outcome of the function of reincarnation. Every incarnation provides different personas, different personalities, different intentions and purposes by which to achieve oneness. Through the multifarious diverse experiences reincarnation provides, you are able to bring more and more of your developing selves to your relationships, and through the resultant harmony you grow spiritually.

So now, what is the connection between diversity and oneness — how are they linked?
The oneness of individuals endowed with free will func-

tions through relationships. Relationships function to create diversity of individuality. Relationships neither start nor end with your present knowledge of them. Their reality continues in both worlds. It is through understanding this continuity that the value of present relationships becomes clear. Present loving relationships build for the future and redeem the past. They seem to come and go, but the continuity of these relationships never ceases.

Do you mean that we reincarnate over and over again with the same people?

We are drawn to them through love, and each time we return it is in a different role in the ongoing story of self development. It is essential to experience both the male and female aspects of incarnate life, as well as married and single, and all nationalities and colors, as they are needed for development.

Although we are required to choose our parents for each incarnation on the basis of what is best for our growth, emotional ties are strong and contribute to decisions about our parental choices and the circumstances that follow. Even though diversity of experience is important to spiritual growth, it is the emotional tie that binds.

The thought of continuing relationships in differing sexes and roles could seem both disturbing and ludicrous to many. What would you say to them?

The more closely you can identify with your eternal selves, the more you will see reincarnation and shifting relationships as opportunities. If you know who you are, you will not feel threatened by the thought, but will know that you are individual and will want to choose to grow. Remember, all who reincarnate have the opportunity to

come prepared to cope with earth life and the consequences of their choice of parents.

Have we been individual from the beginning?

You were created individual. Your individuality is unique
and subject to development. It is purposeful and related
to your final goal. You must come to understand the various elements of your makeup — who you are.

What do you mean by that?

You need to recognize the fundamental differences that
exist between two aspects of your being — your individuality and your personality.

Tell me first about individuality. What is it made up of?

Individuality is that quality that distinguishes you from
all others, God in you (God's Love and God's Will) as it
existed at your creation. It is that intention, that gift, that
wish, that thought of God in you realized.

How do we realize our individuality?

By allowing God in you — your eternal self — to rule your
life. Your individuality develops through reacting constructively and harmoniously to the circumstances of
your life.

Is there a negative side to individuality?

All negation clouds individuality, causing one to become
like all others who have succumbed to negation — deterrent. One's individuality is overshadowed by the clouds
of deterrence losing identity completely. The sun of
God's Will (construction) is the only element that can
disperse the clouds of negation and deterrence, allow-

ing individuality to shine forth nurtured by its healing power.

What about personality?

Your personality changes from incarnation to incarnation depending upon the particular genes you inherit from the parents you have chosen. Your individuality stays with you. You bring what you have earned to each incarnation. Your personality varies with each incarnation. It is the means by which you act out your persona each time. Although it is fleeting, it is meaningful to your development and that of others within your sphere of influence.

Relationships of Blood and Goal

I've been wondering; are there different kinds of relationships? Are they all of equal importance?
There are two fundamental categories of relationships, those of blood and those of goal.

Would you please define them for me?
Relationships of blood include all family relationships — all who are kin. Relationships of goal involve attraction to those known or unknown of similar goal. You are drawn to them, you admire them, you relate to them, you love them in proportion to your development.

Please tell me more about final goals.
Although we have discussed final goals in previous conversations, it would be well to add a word about them.

All forms of life have goals to achieve in each incarnation as they proceed up the ladder of evolution. By the time they become human they are endowed with the specific ultimate goal to which they have been contributing from the beginning. This goal is to be achieved within the conditions of perfect individuality and oneness with God.

There are five ultimate goals: Enlightenment, Teaching, Healing, Leadership, and Creativity. Everyone has one of these as an ultimate goal. We are to be unique elements blending with all other elements of similar goal in an organ of the ever-evolving Body of God.

This identification of ultimate goals is intended merely

to give you a sense of the essence of each. It is impossible to describe their ultimate discarnate function in words that would be understandable to you.

Which are more important, relationships of blood or of goal?

First of all you must realize that all relationships of ultimate merit are of goal. The blood relationships you have from incarnation to incarnation may or may not be of goal. If a family member is close to you emotionally, you can know that that member is also close to you spiritually and is of similar ultimate goal. Those who are not, are not.

But shouldn't we try to make all relationships constructive?

Of course. Harmony is essential to all relationships. However, relationships of goal have the greatest capacity for development.

What is the purpose of the physical basis for relationships?

You are to become involved with and responsible for one another in a compelling and understandable way. You complement one another physically, emotionally, and spiritually. Your physical beings are intertwined. You have all lived in the body of your mothers. You are composed of the genes of your parents, and others may be composed of yours. You are all part of and physically dependent upon the physical whole — water, air, sun, and soil. Your spiritual oneness is a physical reality. You share with others from the moment of your conception.

Just what do you mean by that?

The life in the womb exemplifies the fact that you are

simultaneously independent of and wholly one with your
mother. The sharing process starts with the moment of
conception, which in itself results from the sharing of
bodily functions. The sexual act, when accompanied by
love and caring, lifts you into the most ecstatic state of
unity possible, both emotionally and spiritually. Your
physical existence from the very beginning depends
upon the sharing of basic life elements. Your mother,
your primary sharer, plays a special role in the plan of
your life.

*In what other ways do we share with others phys-
ically?*
You share with others your mental and physical weaknesses and strengths, your genes. You are not separate.

*How does one's sex affect relationships in the
incarnate world?*
Male and female qualities are the expression of God the
Father – Mother on earth. They complement each other
to make a whole, just as the sexual organs complement
each other to make a whole entity, an incarnate individual.

*In what way does each incarnation affect blood
relationships?*
Each incarnation has its own significance in regard to
blood relationships. The heritage and legacy of all previous incarnations play a significant role in the living out
of a particular incarnation. It is what you do about all
that you bring with you that affects your relationships
for good or for ill and through that, your own spiritual
development. Also, it is from the constructive relationships that result from your choice of parents that the
beneficial circumstances of an incarnation develop.

Could there be incarnate life without relationships?
Understand this: Relationships are. Aside from feelings of love, friendship, and compatibility, aside from being drawn to others for unknown reasons, if none of these conditions existed, relationships would still obtain. They are essential ingredients of the incarnate biological process of procreation. These relationships of blood exist in all incarnate life. Every incarnate is a member of an individual family. Although this family changes from incarnation to incarnation, it is distinctly individual each time, offering its own opportunities for growth while remaining an element of the Whole — individuality and oneness joined.

Do we always choose parents of the same goal?
The choice of parents must fulfill a karmic need stemming from former relationships. The purpose is to provide you with the circumstances of life that will help you to grow in that relationship as well as to develop the quality you most need. Whether the choice of parents is wise or unwise cannot be judged by appearances. The previous history of the relationship would have to be known as well as the particular quality you need to develop. You are drawn to the parents who meet your needs, and your needs are responded to. You are drawn together by your need.

Even if it's only what you think you need?
Yes. The need is met and the consequences are yours to live through.

By quality do you mean moral quality?
Yes, and you can see that this could call for inexplicable choices. The need to develop courage for instance, and the choice of a difficult parent bound to you emotion-

ally could have been purposeful in intention, whether or not it was carried out successfully.

That seems to put the burden on the child.

Relationships can be extremely complicated and even disastrous because of emotional decisions or insufficient preparation. However, if both parents and young people would understand that these relationships did not start and will not end with this incarnation, that relationships continue in the unseen as well as the seen world, they would have to face the fact that bringing harmony to all of their relationships is essential to the realization of their ultimate goal.

Goals

How can we utilize our relationships to progress toward our final goal since we are unaware of what it is?

You aren't really. There is a knowledge deep within you — call it a sixth sense — that stirs you, energizes you, moves you emotionally, arouses your desire to create, to heal, to teach, etc. Goals are like a compass — they keep pointing the way.

When you meet someone for instance and there is a spark of recognition, you are probably recognizing your goal in that person.

But there are only a few goals. There must be untold numbers with the same goal to whom I don't relate at all.

You are drawn to a relationship according to your need of the moment. During your multifarious incarnations you have had the opportunity to know a great many. If you don't always relate it is because your present need doesn't include them.

Are there identifying elements in us that designate our goal?

The goal of each of you is made clear in one way or another. For instance, if a man is easy-going and not ambitious, but he loves his family and is generous in his efforts, what do you think his goal might be?

To heal?

Yes, because he is concerned with creating harmony. His wife may wish that he had more ambition, but she loves him for his kindness and consideration.

But how would he know what his goal is?

He acts in accordance with his goal.

Your description of our final goals suggests something much more dynamic than the man you describe.

Not necessarily. You can't judge him. He may be doing very well with the circumstances of his life.

What about an evil man? Does he have a goal too?

He has lost sight of all of that in his preference for hate instead of love. His belief in the will of self instead of the Will of God obliterates his vision.

Could our goal be identified from the characteristics inherited from our parents?

No. To reach your final goal you have many things to overcome and many to gain. Inherited characteristics are merely a means to an end.

So the characteristics inherited from each set of parents provide us with certain elements with which to move forward each time, and these elements contribute to a different set of attributes with which to do the job next time?

That is fundamentally correct. However, you don't change completely each time. Your conscience has been earned from previous incarnations and would be utilized in your present situation along with your spiritual equipment and the elements of development (the circumstances of this incarnation) to come to grips with your present problems. Thus your individuality gradually asserts itself through those elements you have gained along the way.

How would you define conscience?
Your conscience is the faculty you are developing to decide the moral quality of your own thoughts and acts, enjoining what is good, eschewing what is bad through intuition. A developed conscience denotes a developed soul.

But our conscience doesn't define our goal, does it?
No it doesn't. It is a condition of your spiritual development only.

Then if we change in characteristics each time, our way of living could be quite different each time, so where is the common thread of goal?
You would have to examine the results of your efforts each time. "By their fruits shall ye know them." This is certainly true in understanding goals.

Speaking of goals: What is the specific difference between enlightenment and teaching?
Enlightenment has to do with the ability to gain and impart spiritual truths through being. Teaching refers to the ABCs of daily life, those elements that contribute to a life lived in accordance with God's Will. In both of these cases we are discussing goals as they affect a person's conduct during an incarnation. We are not able to describe how goals are applied in the ultimate discarnate state for which they are destined. Those various aspects of which goals are comprised will be so perfected and specialized as to become integral functioning elements of an organ of the body of God.

So it seems we are back to our heart feelings.[1] *We must rely on our true heart feelings to give us clues to our ultimate goal. What we really want in any incarnation contributes to what we will become ultimately?*

Examine your heart and it will lead you to the right path to your goal. Your goal, when finally reached, becomes the realization of your true heart feelings of all of your incarnations. The capacity to reach your goal is present in your spiritual makeup. In consulting your true heart feelings you are consulting your spiritual nature and are therefore in tune with your spirit's aspirations, the ultimate goal of oneness with God. Following your heart feelings develops your true nature, which determines your ultimate goal.

What came first, me or my goal?

Before there was you there was your goal. You emerged from your goal and now exist for your goal. Free will grants you the possibility of deterring the fulfillment of that goal or enhancing it by making it more individual. The individuality that you cultivate emerges from your struggle to do God's Will rather than your own will.

If, for instance, you are trying to solve a problem in a relationship and then suddenly you see the light, you understand the problem, you do the constructive thing — the result is yours. It will always bear the mark of your individuality.

There is no better way to know yourself than by pursuing your relationships utilizing your heart feelings. Your best efforts in this regard indicate most clearly who you are.

---

[1] See *Why You Are Who You Are* (Destiny Books, Rochester, VT 1985).

Please explain this fascinating statement that we emerged from our goal.

The important thing here is to recognize that you are a personification of your goal. God in you is potentially that which, when individualized and perfected, will become a unique irreplaceable element functioning in an organ of the body of God fulfilling God's dream for you.

Are you saying that when God created the angels they were at that point potential aspects of goals to be met that would fulfill His dream?

No, but you are thinking and that's good. Let me say this: The element that you have overlooked is God's Love. Allowing Himself to be made up of multifarious unique individuals, who are at the same time to be one with Him, stems from God's Love. God desired entities of Himself to evolve who would become perfect individuals, unique and still one with Him in the ecstasy of Godhood. This multifaceted realization of God would be comprised of five elements, five organs. Each entity would be a functioning member of one of these five organs.

Did the angels have the same goals as we have?

No. This concept of goals was God's dream of Himself. All of God's creations are products of the concept of goals to be reached to satisfy His dream. The goals of the angels were to create incarnate life forms within the process of evolution, a necessary aspect of incarnate life. All of life, both discarnate and incarnate, is to be one. Each one is to have a special function within this evolving body of God's dream. Those who have chosen to remain discarnate under the influence of God's Will will have their special function, and those that have chosen to utilize their free will, coming to the light of God's Will through evolution by their own choice, will have their special function in the scheme of things. Each specific function is determined by one's choice of path. Those who have taken the path of free will will earn a more complex ultimate function than those who have chosen to remain under God's Will. Also, those of the free will path who have overcome the greatest obstacles will occupy the places of honor — those that are most crucial to the functioning of God's dream body.

When you refer to overcoming the greatest obstacles as a badge of honor, are you saying that we must first have to have been evil and recovered in order to earn God's favor?

The practice of free will involves individual decisions, moral judgements, spiritual growth through one's own efforts. This kind of achievement automatically raises the frequency to a higher level than that which can be achieved under the protection of God's Will alone.

Also the right to make choices implies that wrong as well as right choices will inevitably be made. The more developed one becomes spiritually, the more devastating are sudden compulsive reversions toward evil. The higher the achievement, the lower the depths of degradation. To pull oneself out of this and strive against insurmountable odds to recoup in order to move on and finally overcome takes great stamina, determination, and dedication, and earns a special place in the heart as well as the body of God.

Are you saying that God plays favorites?

Those who have overcome the greatest obstacles, who have had the greatest struggle, earn a place of honor for themselves. They are rewarded for their efforts, the greater the struggle, the greater the reward. This is axiomatic.

*Why should we know about goals since they affect
us so little now?*

If you were to believe that many of your meaningful relationships had the same goal, would that affect your attitude toward them?

I don't see how.

Well, think of this: What you do every day is colored by
your relationships. If you knew that you and these others
were going to end up together in complete harmonious
perfection, would that affect your attitude toward them
now?

*I guess that I would feel that the more we work for
harmony now, the better for all in the future.*

You are thinking well.

*Of all our relationships of goal, what determines
those to whom we are particularly drawn?*

You will be drawn only to those within your own sphere
of influence and those whose development causes the
magnetic quality of the goal to be felt. You may not necessarily find all of them agreeable because there are too
many other factors involved. But those to whom you do
respond can tell you a great deal about yourself.

Is our choice of parents always dependent on goal?

Your choice is dependent upon you. It may or may not
be entirely in accordance with goal, although it generally is.

Choice of parents must be considered more carefully
now. In the first place, are we talking about parents or
parent? Ideally it is the former, but that is seldom possible. Your need to join, to become a part of a particular
person is the compelling factor. Once having found that

person, you need to consider his or her spouse as well. This could rule out the choice, but not necessarily.

Therefore, one of your parents as well as subsequent siblings need not be of your goal. In the course of a life you can therefore become bound to those of other goals.

As I consider the list of goals I can find many to which I relate.
But you have chosen to do this work. Doesn't that tell you something?

It seems closest to Enlightenment, but I've spent most of my life teaching.
Which demonstrates an important point: It is important not to be too literal in your thinking. Before you reach your final goal you may tread many different paths, have rough terrain to cross, experience extreme difficulties, have wonderful adventures. You may lose your way and find it over and over again, but whatever happens, you have your spiritual equipment to guide you. This is beautifully and graphically told in our fairy stories, our myths, and our legends.

Are we really to believe the myths and legends to be true?
You are in grave danger of losing your sense of truth if you insist that nothing is true unless proven true. What an absurdity when you can only prove what exists in the seen world! Can you imagine that truth exists anywhere except in God? Those who come nearest to it are those who live most intuitively, those who are able to function so simply that their final goal is clearly identifiable. Their lives affect the Whole constructively.

I suppose that you refer to the prophets, to the great revealers of truth?

Yes, but such lofty phrases are unnecessary. Advanced souls come in all walks of life, as scientists, artists, teachers, ordinary men and women. Paradoxically, the more they have been a part of the Whole, the more they have done God's Will, the more individual they are. It is through the efforts of all such people that a new understanding will grow. Out of the need to relate to one another and the life-giving earth of which you are a part, you come to see yourself and your goal as part of the Whole.

Spiritual achievement is not blending into the Will of God, but rather forging a unique, totally individual entity through which God's Will functions freely.

Environs

What do my environs have to do with sharing?
The earth is your physical home. You wouldn't be you
without your environs — earth, air, water, and sun, and
all that are nourished by them.

When you respect all living things, you respect yourself. When you defile them, you defile yourself. By realizing that all other living things have just as much right
to the blessings of the earth as you do, you recognize that
you are all part of the Whole — God.

In what manner do my environs make me me?
Through your reactions with the circumstances of your
life, which include your environs. You are all incarnate
manifestations of discarnate conceptions. All that exists
on earth is related to all else as different elements of the
incarnate world, each element essential to the complete
functioning of life on earth.

*Are all incarnate manifestations essential to the
function of earth life, or are some of them just the
result of discarnate fantasy?*
It is all integral and essential to the well-being of life on
earth. All matter contains life, and all life is part of the
source of life — God. Therefore rational beings are to
understand their relationship to all else and their obligation to the welfare of others. This includes you yourself.

You tend to think of beastiality as a deterrent element in your nature. But there is no beast to be found that would act toward its own as sadistically as humans can act toward each other. The diabolic fiendish scheming of humans against humans results unfortunately from the granting of free will to God's rational beings. You must recognize that the innocence of all other living creatures functioning through instinct keeps them aloof fi om any form of evil. In recognizing this, you should work through your own rational nature to emulate that state of being with your own free will.

Why should we want to do this?

With the establishment of evolution and reincarnation (the evolution of the spirit), you who are still experiencing the growth cycles are the result of God's continuing desire to create. You started as sparks of life from which you have evolved. You must realize therefore that you have been innocent animals yourselves, and so it is important to recognize potential humans in all animals, treating them with the respect they are due. You should utilize your free will responsibly.

Since many species of life on earth have already become extinct through human willfulness and many more are on the endangered list, how does this speak for us?

This is only one of the many examples of the way human beings have devastated and continue to devastate their home. If you don't soon learn to recognize yourselves as part of the Whole and protect other living things, regarding them as essential to the function of earth life, you will find yourselves responsible for the undoing of God's plan and deterring God's dream for us all.

How would we be undoing the plan of reincarnation by these actions?

By causing the extinction of so many species of God's creation, mankind is effectively eliminating opportunities for evolutionary growth, and thus limiting valuable experiences afforded by the distinctive qualities of species that are necessary to the successful evolution of souls. As this devastation continues, the process becomes more and more limited. Each species has a different purpose in the function of evolution, and the elimination of any one can cause a rift in the weaving of the web of God's dream.

The Whole

Exactly how do we share with others emotionally?
You share through function. As a part of the Whole, your function is always in relationship to others. You cannot separate it from others. Just as you are part of others physically, so you are part of others emotionally. It is a great emotional ecosystem that functions as the physical one does in accordance with the law of cause and effect.

What would you say is the significance of this?
Nothing happens by chance. All relationships are purposeful, including those in the unseen as well as the seen world. It is your job to discover their karmic significance and fulfill it. Belief in the reality of those in the unseen world will help you to live in the seen world.

How does this great emotional ecosystem function?
Through your relationships. It is the way that you *feel* about someone or something that really affects your spiritual development, rather than the way you *think* about them.

Could you say then that it is our emotional life rather than our intellectual life that is the basis of our spiritual progress and is therefore superior to it?
You could.

31

But isn't emotion the result of thought? Don't we think before we react, so that thought and emotion are paired?

It is true that thought can precede action when you consider negative emotions. You may think hateful thoughts before you feel hatred. However, when it comes to love (the only emotion that is of God), it and all of its aspects, including sympathy, empathy, understanding, attachment, affection, benevolence, adoration, tenderness, passion, consideration, long-suffering, patience, tolerance, etc., are prompted by intuition. Love does not and cannot stem from a mental process. It is motivated by the intuitive sense of the spirit — God within.

It would seem then that our emotional life is the most important element of our incarnate experience.

You are correct, and since it is expressed within your relationships it has the greatest effect upon them.

You say that we are part of others emotionally. Could you describe how this functions?

For example, you and I are strongly attached emotionally because of our close relationship over many many incarnations. This has been of blood and is constantly of goal. When I say a strong emotional relationship, I refer to the sharing of feelings — those joys, those sorrows, those aspirations, those discouragements, those discoveries, those desires, and your love — those feelings that are the basis of your spiritual growth.

However, when we discuss human feelings, we must include all the negative feelings, all the hateful feelings, all the envious feelings, and all of the fearful feelings. Remember, it is not the thought itself that affects you one way or the other, it is the feeling that it provokes that determines your spiritual path. If you are traveling the path of negativism, you are causing ruptures in your relationships that must be repaired if you are to proceed on the path of construction. This condition is a cry for help, and the response is crucial to the outcome of a relationship.

Can those who respond really benefit the situation?

Those who are close to you emotionally, who work to heal your self-inflicted wounds, can bring you into the light of clear thinking. In so doing they are expressing loyalty — they are being loyal to you. Loyalty is that aspect of love that serves to cement relationships. It keeps them constant through thick and thin. It relates them to your allegiance to God, resulting in great benefit.

Isn't physical violence just as devastating to a relationship as negativism?

You are all capable of affecting others by your emotions in an even more telling way than by physical means. Your social life and your emotional life go hand in hand. All relationships have an emotional basis to one degree or another. The very term "relationship" implies the involvement of emotional values, to which you may add physical values and from which you can gain spiritual values.

But isn't physical violence the result of emotional upheaval?

Yes, it is. But no matter how destructive the physical violence may be, it is the emotion behind it that can truly devastate relationships. Emotional damage is more telling, has more lasting results than physical damage. The effect may be physical, but the cause is emotional.

Can expressing our emotions benefit us spiritually?
It is only love that creates harmony in relationships and
raises the frequency of those involved. All other emotions stem from self-will generating disharmony in relationships, thus lowering the frequency of those involved.

*I am struck by how apt the verb "to share" is in con-
sidering ourselves and our environment. Sharing
is essential to God's plan.*
You should now try to consider just what you have said.
Of what does sharing consist?

*I think that sharing means both giving and receiv-
ing, and since we have learned that giving and
receiving are the same, this must be sharing. Then
the greatest act of sharing must have been God's
granting of free will to human beings enabling us
to share the Godhead. It is not only that we do share
with others on a physical level, but that we must
consciously share on an emotional level too.*
You see now that you are to bring sharing into every element of your life to emphasize your individuality and
your oneness. In the conscious act of sharing, you are
giving of your individuality and making it part of the
Whole. Your individuality becomes an element of the
Whole. You are fulfilling your birthright.

*Could you say also that we share our deterrent qual-
ities?*
No. You never share deterrence. You impose deterrence
upon others, causing them difficulties as well as yourself. Sharing is an act of love. Imposing is an act of hate.

Is there more to be said about sharing?
Examine the word and any possible connotations it may
have for you.

I think that relationships themselves imply sharing and to the extent to which they are of blood or goal, these elements within a relationship are shared. However, I can think of many reasons why I may not share or desire to share love or anything else within a relationship. Do we have to love, or even like, all of our relations of blood or of goal?

If two people just have a shared relationship of blood or of goal, is that sufficient? What is the ultimate purpose of such relationships?

Shouldn't I be asking you these questions?

I want you to answer them.

Well, I suppose that since our relationships of blood and goal are irrevocable, and since the purpose of all relationships is to lead us to our relationship to the Whole (God), and since this cannot come about without love, it behooves us then to consciously bring harmony into these relationships so there can be a total sharing, each with the other and with the Whole.

Some elements of our relationships result from the circumstances of our lives and some elements from our reactions to these circumstances.

Are these thoughts acceptable to you?

Yes, but I'd like to add this:

Sharing includes retaining one's core. You must always retain something to share. In the act of sharing you are never to lose sight of your identity, but give and receive as part of the Whole recognizing this as essential to God's plan for you.

Sharing in itself is an act of love, and without love you fail in your relationship with the Whole. It is the function of one who is both individual and one with God. In sharing with others you acknowledge your relationship to them and to God. As God shares His Will with you, so you are to share your will with Him (the Whole). In this way God's kingdom will manifest itself on earth through your efforts. God's faith in you will have been justified, and God's dream will ultimately come about.

Must all relationships be brought to this state?

Yes. Through the act of sharing you move yourself forward in your spiritual development, and by so doing you help others on their way. The act of sharing embodies love. No relationship, however casual, is complete without some manifestation of a facet of love.

You can learn to see yourself more clearly as you work to eliminate your faults and work out your newly acquired qualities within a loving relationship. In this way you are able to complete an incarnation on a higher level of frequency than you started. It all turns on the act of sharing.

I'd like you to try to think of other important verbs that affect the outcome of an incarnation.

I can think of to hope and to have faith, since it is through our hope that God approves of our actions and through our faith in the goodness of God that we become God-centered and are freed to share with others unequivocally. I guess our sharing would be incomplete without the freedom generated by hope and faith.

You now understand the importance of sharing.

How can we learn to understand the Whole?

To begin to understand the Whole you must first understand your whole self. Not just the person of this incarnation, but the self you were before birth and will be after death; your true self; God in you; that which is individual and also one, occupying one world.

What do you mean by one world?
The same laws govern the seen and the unseen. It is all one world. You and I live in different aspects of the same world, the same space, differing only in frequency — a difference that can be equalized not only through prayer or communication, but even by sight, sound, and touch. Every thought and deed in one world has repercussions in the other. Positive thoughts and actions set Constructive Force in motion; negative thoughts and actions set Deterrent Force in motion in both worlds.

Responsibility for one another is no different here or there. Relationships are always unfinished. What animates them here continues there, and what animates them there continues here.

Since continuing relationships — in fact life itself — are made possible in the incarnate world by sex, is there an equivalent condition in the discarnate world?
Not in the sense of procreation. But male and female qualities stem from God the Father – Mother, and exist in essence through the Whole. In order to experience and understand both aspects of the Whole, you reincarnate sometimes as male and sometimes as female depending upon the relationship you need to develop.

In the Place of Preparation do we retain the elements of our previous incarnate sex, or do we revert to our angelic qualities?
You retain each time the elements that were dominant in your previous incarnation, the qualities of maleness or femaleness. This is signified both by color and intensity, elements of forcefulness or receptivity. In the ultimate state both elements will have become fully developed and perfected. Nothing happens by chance. Everything has a purpose. Just as you must develop both the male

and female aspects with which you were created, so you must also develop the qualities needed to fulfill your final goal. The purpose of each incarnation is to develop a particular quality through your relationships utilizing your spiritual equipment. Each quality developed leads you nearer to your final goal — a functioning element of the Whole — one with God.

Spiritual Equipment

What is the substance of our spiritual equipment?
It is made of elements of God. These three God-elements are present in everyone — love, sense of truth, and intuition. They have been a part of you prior to your first incarnate experience.

Would you please define them for me?
Your love is the essence of God's gift of Himself, particularized.

Your sense of truth is the ability to differentiate between what is right and what is wrong for you, to know when your will is or is not God's Will. You accomplish this by searching your heart.

Your intuition is the ability to just know without reasoning. This comes from aligning yourself with your discarnate nature (your soul), thus extending yourself into the discarnate world.

How do we extend ourselves into the discarnate world?
At first it is through the process of concentrated imagination, imagining yourself in your discarnate state. Imagination is the bridge between the worlds.

As you seek the solution to a problem of relationships in this imaginative state, your intuition is freed to respond to your needs shedding light on the solution. It could be very different from the one you might think of

because the mind is not to be trusted to know what is
best in such situations.

How would we go about imagining ourselves in the discarnate state?

There are many ways of achieving this, but let me give
you an example of a way to begin.

Lie down flat on a bed or couch, close your eyes and
gradually sense yourself sinking deeper and deeper into
the bed or couch until you become a part of it. Make sure
that you are feeling utterly comfortable lying there. You
must be totally relaxed or this process won't work. Then
set your spirit free, imagining it hovering over you. This
you are to recognize as the spiritual you, the source of
love and truth with whom you are to feel free to discuss
your problems knowing that your freed mind will be able
to receive truth.

This process is not easily accomplished. So much
depends upon the use of your imagination and your ability to concentrate. However, the more you use this process to solve your problems, the sooner you will be able
to free yourself from this concentrated imagining, putting yourself readily into the discarnate atmosphere
before considering a problem that needs solving, until
finally you will find your intuition responding with alac-
rity to your problems as you consider them.

When you speak of spiritual equipment are you talking about the functioning factors of our eternal beings?

Yes I am. You need to see that the fundamental task of
all incarnates is to relate to these faculties of their discarnate eternal beings, making them theirs through use.

But since our elements of development are the cir-

cumstances of our lives, they are also to be used, aren't they?

The circumstances of your life — the traits and personality you have inherited by your choice of parents, the environment into which you are born, etc. — are the conditions through which you function from day to day, utilizing your spiritual equipment as needed. How you use these elements determines your spiritual development.

Are you saying that these circumstances of our lives become the elements of our development when they are used to uncover and utilize our spiritual equipment?

Exactly. Your spirituality grows and develops through the use of your spiritual equipment. The circumstances of your life determine where, with whom, and with what you are to function on earth. But it is from within these circumstances that your spiritual equipment is to be brought forth and utilized in all of your relationships. Your love, your sense of truth, and your intuition are able to foster as well as mend all relationships, guiding you toward your goal not only for an incarnation, but also for your ultimate state of being. Without the use of this equipment no spiritual progress can be made. It is your spiritual equipment that identifies you as a spiritual being.

How are we able to recognize our spiritual equipment?

By following your heart feelings and examining yourself to uncover your inner needs. Although these subjects have been covered extensively before,[1] let me say that

---

[1] See *Why You Are Who You Are* (Destiny Books, Rochester, VT, 1985).

by learning to trust your inner heart feelings where God dwells and knowing what you really want, you can bring your spiritual equipment to the surface to be used as the modus operandi of your life. As this takes place you will be gradually functioning according to plan, growing spiritually. You may find, however, that one element of your spiritual equipment is more dominant than the others, putting you off balance spiritually. For example, there are some who are giving and loving but find it difficult to see the truth in situations because they trust their minds to solve their problems, overlooking or ignoring their intuition entirely. Love will be limited by this oversight and possibly short-lived.

Others may have a highly developed sense of truth but are not motivated by love or intuition. And there are those who are highly developed intuitively who possess a sixth sense about things, but unless this too is motivated by love and balanced by a sense of truth, they will not be functioning fully according to God's Will.

In order to do God's Will as planned, all three elements of your spiritual equipment are to be put to use.

Why are we generally out of balance in the use of our spiritual equipment?

That has to do with capacity.

What do you mean by that?

Capacity refers to the way you have lived — whether or not you have made use of your spiritual equipment during your various incarnations by learning to know yourself each time, searching your heart, examining your inner feelings, and whether or not you are doing so now. As you do this your spiritual capacity to function increases through the use of your love, sense of truth, and intuition. Otherwise this equipment lies dormant, availing you nothing.

Since we have this spiritual equipment, why don't we know more about it?

Because each time you return the curtain is drawn on your memory and you are required once more to search your heart for what is buried there, learning about your needs and desires and living in faith. It should be remembered that this equipment is a gift from God for you to use. You are the final arbiter. You must figure out each time what these elements are telling you and put them to use as required.

Why is it that our spiritual equipment doesn't seem to be equal for all?

Because everyone is unique and spiritual equipment is an element of individuality. The proportion of each can vary with individual use. This has to do with the natural inclination of one's individuality resulting from long experience and practice. To grow spiritually one must grow with equanimity. A highly developed soul has all three elements in equal proportion.

Please give me an example of how we put our spiritual equipment to use.

Let us say that two people have fallen in love and want to marry but their sense of truth tells them that everything is against it. They're from different backgrounds, different faiths, so it can't possibly work. However, even though their families and friends advise against it, they both sense intuitively (they just *know*) that the strength and depth of their love will be able to overcome all apparent objections and will prevail in spite of all. But their sense of truth has done its job too by preparing them to face facts and put matters in their proper perspective.

In the same set of circumstances, if both of them were to recognize serious problems, causing them to become uneasy and tentative, they would intuitively be feeling that something most certainly was wrong. It could be that they are interpreting physical attraction and sensuality as love, that they are not truly in love after all, and that there is another plan for their lives. In any case it is they who must decide.

This all sounds very complicated.

Sometimes the job of arbiter *is* very complicated, especially when there are conflicting claims on your emotions such as a decision regarding a marriage separation when children are involved. It can help in such a situation to bring each aspect of your spiritual equipment to the surface, coping with each separately, and then trying to balance them.

Your love will tell you what you really care about, what your heart feelings are; your sense of truth will inform you of the reality of the situation, what is right to do; and your intuition will sense how you should proceed to achieve a constructive outcome.

In order to utilize your spiritual equipment a constant overlay of emotion must be cleared away. Your effort to accomplish this activates the Law of Parallels, giving you new energy and faith to make the proper decisions, and this, in turn, will result in a better balance and increased capacity in the use of your spiritual equipment.

II. The Function of Relationships

Who Are You?

Why don't we know more about our former lives and relationships?

You *do* know. The eternal you is fully aware of all your lives. This is true whether you are in the seen or unseen world. However, in the seen world this specific knowledge doesn't usually reach the level of consciousness. There are exceptions, but they aren't germane to this discussion.

Why aren't we conscious of our past lives?

Because the important elements of incarnate life are to learn to live in faith in the goodness of God, and to know that nothing that happens to you is as important as what you think about it. There are no accidents. All events are meaningful. By accepting yourself for who you are and perceiving your development for what it is, you know all that is necessary for you to know about your past lives.

If the incarnate me is unaware of my past lives, what do I gain by being told that the eternal me does know?

The eternal you can influence your thoughts and actions if you are able to allow it to rule your life. This influence is based on the knowledge of how your reactions to former events influence your present decisions, and how to set matters straight.

How do I get my eternal self to rule me?

By bringing yourself back to your heart feelings you are revealing the wishes of God in you. When you obey these feelings you are being ruled by your eternal self.

How do I gain the knowledge that my former reactions affect my present decisions?

Through the belief that your present proclivities are the result of the past, you come to see how your past has influenced your present. The way you feel about something or someone, your reason for wanting to do something, your interest in certain matters, and your complete lack of interest in, or even revulsion toward, others: these are all indications of what has been gleaned from past lives. You see that your present is the result of the past.

But we do know our past lives when we are in the unseen world, don't we?

In the Place of Preparation you do learn about your past lives. In this aspect of reality you know your complete history — all you have been from the inception of your individuality. There it becomes your job to deal with the result of your past incarnate life and to prepare for the next one, beginning with the most important relationships, your parents: just who they will be.

What does this choice do for us?

On earth you are to carry out the intention with which you were born. You are now to make it so. Your total concentration is on one life — the relationships with which you are involved in this life, the quality or qualities you came to develop this time, the karmic faults you must deal with, and the circumstances in which you find yourself.

Because you have chosen to do so of your own free will, you are free to develop either in accordance with God's Will or your own will.

I still think it would be helpful to know more about our former selves here and now.

It might interest you and in some instances it is helpful, but it is at best fragmentary and not necessarily in the plan of incarnate life.

Why?

Reincarnation came about in response to need. It is difficult enough to try to fulfill one life and the relationships that are part of that life. If you were to become aware of the complexity and emotional impact of all of your lives and relationships in any depth, you would find them impossible to cope with. However, you already do know and can discover all you need to know if you know yourself.

Are you speaking of the personal unconscious as described in psychology?

No. The information in the personal unconscious is not easily available to everyone because it is revealed in terms of symbols. Symbols are a sort of psychic shorthand, often needing interpretation. However, there are more accessible ways for you to learn who you are as a result of who you have been.

What does our present indicate to us about our past?

You are a product of your past, the result of everything you have been. You *are* your past, but in saying this it is necessary to be clear about your character and the circumstances of your life.

What must we know about our character?

Your character is the essential you — that which you would be no matter what the circumstances of your life were. It is your character that is your inheritance from your former lives.

How did we arrive at this essential being?

Through your efforts to achieve your goal at each incarnation.

Please describe character to me.

Your character is the aggregate of the qualities you have earned, a stamp of your individuality. It is earned from incarnation to incarnation through the use of love, the sense of truth, and intuition — your spiritual equipment. When fully realized it will become an essential element of your final goal.

Of what exactly is our character comprised?

It is comprised of your traits and qualities, including moral strength, self discipline, and fortitude — those things that become permanent elements of your individuality as a result of your constructive efforts.

What is the process through which we develop character?

It is through reactions to your various relationships that your character is built. The circumstances of your life and the events that culminate from them offer you opportunities to grow in accordance with your reactions to them. Relationships are integral to this growth. In developing the qualities you came to acquire, you are developing your character.

There must be a negative side to this.

Every positive has a negative. One's character could

include moral weakness and a total lack of fortitude and self-discipline stemming from following self-will and the deterrence that results. You must determine for yourself just where you fit into this picture, what kind of character you have developed, and then act on it remembering that it is your character that you take with you.

What about the circumstances of life?

The circumstances of each life are what you have been given as a result of your choice of parents in a particular incarnation. They become your elements of development.

What specifically do elements of development refer to?

The term implies that the circumstances of your relationships are intended to develop you and move you forward spiritually, raising your frequency in the process. Each incarnation is meant to count for something. You realize your elements of development by acting constructively toward your relationships, living according to God's Will.

What do our relationships indicate about us?

The knowledge that they are elements of the circumstances of your life that you yourself have chosen through your choice of parents should be sobering. Since you have chosen them, you are responsible for their welfare as they are for yours. Your primary concern is to create harmony in your relationships in an effort to undo past wrongs or build upon past strengths, and learn to grow through them. It is valuable to realize that all relationships are useful in this way. Understanding that your present relationships did not start and will not end with

this life offers clues to the quality of your former lives and
what you want for your future lives.

Are we to learn from and grow through all *of our present relationships?*

Casual relationships of the moment don't necessarily
carry much importance, but relationships of blood or
goal most certainly do. They are eternal bonding factors
that cannot be denied. Your actions and reactions within
these relationships determine the rate and quality of
growth toward your ultimate goal. And if you will examine your daily life with this in mind, you can learn much
about where you stand now.

Just what should we know about ourselves?

Begin actually by imagining that you are part of God's
evolving Will. This involves you historically, geographically, and genetically.

Historically you are part of the past. You have a personal history, a continuing thread weaving in and out
of the pattern of world history. Geographically you have
lived not only in many parts of the seen world, but also
in the unseen. You relate to both. You have a dual cit-
izenship. Genetically you are a seed containing past
and future relationships while retaining your original
potential.

Can I learn more about being a seed containing both past and future relationships?

Past and future relationships exist in the present. In your
present behavior you reflect what you have gained from
the past and also what you are contributing to your
future. Your future becomes the result of your reactions
to events in the present. This seed will come to fruition
when you have finally achieved your purpose.

How can we understand our purpose this time?

By learning to identify the qualities you need to develop. In seeing the qualities you lack you will come to know what you have failed to do and must now do for your future growth.

Does being part of God's evolving Will have any special significance for our future growth?

God has willed you to become a part of Him. You would not exist but for this fact. This element of God's dream was so important that, after the granting of free will failed to achieve the inherent results because of the proclivity toward deterrence, God then created the perfect solution to the problems providing another opportunity to accomplish His dream. Responsibility functioning through reincarnation became the issue that was new, requiring humans to rely solely on their spiritual equipment to reach their goal.

You say that historically we are part of the past. What is the importance of this statement?

What is important is the fact that you *are*. Being, in this sense, implies that you have always been, that you have evolved, become innocently obedient to God's Will, succumbed to the temptations of self-will, and are now attempting to work yourself out of your problems in an effort to reach your ultimate goal. All of this involves a past, a present, and even a future.

Some say that the past and the future are all one, a part of the present — that they are all going on simultaneously. How do you answer this? Are our past and our future going on now?

You have asked a complicated question. All life exists in

the present. Your past, what you remember of it, exists for you only as you ponder it in the present.

I don't think you answered my question.

Just hold on, I haven't finished yet. To the degree that you live in the present, not regretting or longing for the past or anticipating the future, you are living past, present, and future all at once. Your present is the product of the past, and your future will result from the present. Therefore, if you concentrate on the present, you will be including your past and your future.

But haven't you said that there is indeed no past or future on your side, only the present?

Yes, I have. Your time and our time are not the same. You live by sidereal time. We do not. But living in the moment puts you in our time. The only time either of us experiences is *now.*

Just how does being responsible to all our relationships, past and present, spell out?

Your relationships are not past and present. They are all present. Some of them are incarnate and some of them are discarnate, but they all exist now. Your primary responsibility is to your family and loved ones on earth, but you also have a responsibility to those relationships who are not on earth. You are to pray for those whom you remember, and also ask them to pray for you.

You should give thought to the fact that there are many, many relationships, both incarnate and discarnate, that you do not at present have any memory of. You do, however, have responsibility for the souls involved in those relationships. They remain your relationships and are affected by what you think and do in some way too. Refer to them in your prayers as your relationships that you do not at present remember, showing your sense of responsibility toward them as well. In this way you learn to live in both worlds.

I understand this continuing thread as a concept, but what does it mean to me in practical terms?

It means that your life has been involved with many, many other lives in the endless time you have been evolving as a human. It means that the interplay of your relationships has formed patterns woven into the tapestry of incarnate life, and will continue to do so as you choose incarnate life again and again.

Your pattern, comprised of your own thread interwoven with threads of your relationships, appears whenever you are in the incarnate state. While you are in the discarnate state your thread will not be detected in the tapestry, although many of your relationships who had been a part of your pattern will continue forming other patterns as long as they remain incarnate, their particular threads continuing to be woven with others.

The pattern of your presence on earth is created by your reaction to events surrounding you and your efforts involving your relationships. As they evolve, the pattern varies in symmetry and color depending upon how well you live out a particular incarnation. Some of the patterns may be bright and intricately complex, while others may be dull or simple. In whatever guise, still you are there making your contribution to the tapestry of history.

In practical terms this tells you that everyone is as important to God as everyone else and that your efforts either do or do not contribute to the harmony of the Whole. Either your efforts fulfill God's Will and contribute to your spiritual growth and that of your relationships, or they don't. That is up to you.

You say that geographically we have lived many places including both worlds. Since we are not aware of this, what importance does it have for us?
The reason that you have lived all over the seen world is to experience relationships in all possible ways and under all possible conditions. In order to mend past relationships or to build upon them, you find yourself sometimes in the same place with the same people, but more often in a different place with a different nationality and race. Since you grow spiritually through your relationships, you are to experience whatever environment is necessary to do so.

Do we travel around the unseen world too?
You can do so within the limitations determined by frequency. You go to the place (frequency) you have earned. In the Place of Preparation you work on your needs as you see them, renewing relationships with those who are there, getting a glimpse of what is in store for you in the Realms. Here you remain working on your needs until you decide you are willing and able to reincarnate.

It is the Place of Preparation in the unseen world that is really home to you. Your relationships have grown and developed through your efforts in the unseen world, and as a result you have become a citizen of both worlds. You have spent much more time with your loved ones in the unseen world than in the seen world. However, the seen world is an experience of tremendous essential importance to your development. Through life on earth you give permanence to the qualities you need for spiritual growth toward your goal.

Are there other ways of identifying ourselves?
Identifying your good and your bad karma — your assets and your liabilities — helps you to understand who you

have been and now are in regard to your relationships with others. Without realizing it you describe aspects of karma in your everyday speech. For instance, "He is at peace with himself," or "She is her own worst enemy."

An integrated person is one who is coping with the ramifications of karmic heritage. Intense personal feelings of antipathy or sympathy are strong clues as to whether or not a relationship is to be a continuing one and whether it should be taken seriously. If you just can't get along with some family member, if you find it difficult to forgive, ask yourself why — just as you should if you are unaccountably drawn to others who become close friends.

Couldn't antipathy exist in a relationship of goal too?

Yes, it could. However, such feelings are also mixed with feelings of love if the relationship is truly meaningful. A love – hate relationship is common to much unresolved karma. Antipathy of itself is fundamentally a no-growth condition.

What do our close friends tell us about ourselves?

They tell you that you are a part of them and they are a part of you. Through your close friends with whom you share your close feelings, aspirations, and realizations, your joys and your sorrows, with whom you agree and disagree, but with whom you remain close nonetheless, it is possible to learn much about yourself. Through the substance, quality, and vitality of these relationships you can discover more about your present state of development.

What is the substance, quality, and vitality of friendship?

The substance of friendship is mutual understanding and respect — aspects of love.

The quality of friendship is compatibility.

The vitality of friendship is derived from shared interests.

I can see all that we share with our close friends not only contributes a great deal toward an understanding of our own development up to now, but since they have become and always will be a part of us they can tell us a great deal about our future.

How do those to whom we're attracted help to define us?

First of all, how would you define attraction?

I guess it would be those who interest us.

I think you will find yourself attracted to others for reasons other than simple interest.

Then how would you define our attractions?

Let us define your attractions as those you admire, those who engage your interest sexually, those who inspire you, those to whom you reach out, those who fascinate you, and finally those with whom you have an affinity in the present or have had an affinity in the past, seen or unseen.

What does this tell us?

It tells you that your attractions can help you see both constructive and deterrent elements in yourself. If you admire or are inspired by works of great artists, that tells you that you appreciate the value of talent and effort of one kind. If you admire and are inspired by stock market manipulators, that tells you that you appreciate the value of talent and effort of quite another kind. Ask yourself what kind of person engages your interest, fascinates you, who those are with whom you feel an affinity — your kindred souls.

How would you define kindred souls?

This can be anyone from the person you are destined to fall in love with and spend your life with, to someone you know from reading about, or to the creator of a work of art to which you are unaccountably drawn. Why are you inspired by a particular person? Why does another person make you feel more alive? These are those to whom you feel kindred and they can tell you a great deal about yourself, present and past. This is the best way for you to begin to understand your own final goal because it is fundamentally that in kindred souls to which you are drawn.

It seems to me we're involving self-examination here.

Yes, exactly. Self-examination should be an ongoing effort because the answers to self-probing enable you to understand yourself and the qualities you need in your relationships in order to move forward spiritually. This process has been discussed before.[1] However, you should try to identify your needs first by recognizing your problems.

Your problems can be identified by answering the question, "What do I really want and need?" Search your heart to learn what it tells you about this. It will take persistent probing to get at the right answers. You must of course learn to separate your true heart's desires from compulsive desire and needs. Remember, your heart is where God in you dwells — your temple of truth. Your true heart feelings will be found as you search your heart and recognize that they are totally different from your compulsions. In this way you separate the qualities you

---

[1] See *Why You Are Who You Are* (Destiny Books, Rochester, VT, 1985).

need from your karmic problems, and you discover that your compulsions are what you don't really want. To recognize the difference is a mark of development.

What can those who are unseen indicate about us?
Consider those to whom you have been related, but have gone on.

What are we to think about them?
Well, what do you think about them? Do you remember them? Do you think of them as still living and related to you? Do you pray for them and their progress and development? Do you talk to them or do you think of them as in the past and gone, no longer a part of your life? After all, once you're dead you're dead! Your reactions to these questions can tell you much about your spiritual development and understanding.

I can understand communication. After all, that's what we're up to now. But what do you mean by just talking to those on the other side?
By talking I mean, of course, directing your thoughts toward them. Believe me when I say that if you purposefully direct your thoughts — your prayers, your hopes, your interest, and your love — toward those who have gone on, they will receive your messages and be grateful for them even though they don't answer you. Your thoughts are received by them as sparks of light, electric currents containing your messages. Even if you merely direct your attention toward them they receive the sparks and know from whom they come. Also, it is possible to ask them to pray for you just as you pray for them. Great benefit can be derived on both sides from such activity, resulting in the raising of frequency.

Even though you may feel closer to those relationships

that you remember, inside or outside of your present sphere of influence, still you owe allegiance to all of your relationships seen or unseen, known or unknown. You have had at one time an active relationship with them and you will again if need be, so a bond remains intact that is to be acknowledged. For this reason you owe them your allegiance. You are to refer to them as your relationships that you don't at present remember. In this way you come to feel yourself as a part of the Whole including all of those with whom you have had incarnate relationships who are now discarnate.

I assume that since construction begets construction, deterrence must beget deterrence?
As you sow, so shall you reap. The law of cause and effect functions continuously in the seen world, the unseen world, and between the seen and the unseen worlds.

I suppose that since our previous deterrent relationships have resulted in our present karmic problems, we are reminded of them through their manifestations. I see that past construction would work the same way.
Your conclusions are accurate.

Is it possible that even a prevailing negative attitude could come from former deterrent relationships on earth?
That is what your karma is all about. Your attitude of mind, either deterrent or constructive, is a karmic result of your reactions to your relationships in previous lives. Deterrent reactions would build up a preponderance of negativism that would need to be eradicated before spiritual progress could develop. Everyone must learn the value of construction, and that means construction in all relationships.

Does the good we gain always come from what we have done in the past?

It comes from both your past and your present reactions.

How could one know whether the benefit is derived from a previous incarnation or the present one?

This has to do with magnitude. If the good deeds have been many and of long standing, if they have resulted from the constructive atmosphere that has surrounded the person over many incarnations, the effects will likewise be many and of long duration, on into ensuing incarnations. If the good has resulted from modest day-to-day efforts, the effect will be modest good in return as the person proceeds with an incarnation. There can be both short- and long-term effects from both beneficent and detrimental causes of sufficient magnitude.

Is it really not possible to learn about ourselves from our past lives?

How you lived, where you lived, and who you were in your multifarious past lives is basically unimportant. What is important here however, is whether or not you have succeeded or failed in your efforts toward your goal. The very thought of having lived in the past brings you to the conclusion that your present state is the result of your past.

When you examine yourself you recognize your faults and your assets, your debits and your credits, and you see that in the past you've both failed and succeeded in your efforts (your karma, bad or good). If you are able to see yourself clearly you can arrive at a sense of proportion, the degree to which you have succeeded or failed in working toward construction. Are you grateful for those former selves of yours or do you wish they had done better? The answers to these questions will

reveal to you still another important consideration
—your future.

What do you mean?

Since you realize that your present self is the result of
your past, you also must realize that your future self will
result from your present. How does that make you feel
about your future?

*It makes me recognize how important my present
is to me; how responsible I am, here and now, for my
future. What I think and do from moment to moment
affects my future incarnations. But this seems like
a very heavy load to carry. Am I allowed no leeway
for error?*

You learn about yourself from your errors. Without error
you would not be human. What matters ultimately is the
result of an incarnation, the balance between construction and deterrence. Realizing that your future behavior
is determined by your present behavior gives you an
added incentive to try harder to do what you know is
right, to react constructively to the events of your life,
and to accept your present relationships as right for your
growth and development. You alone are responsible for
your progress. It is only through your efforts that God
can be present on earth. You must be mindful of this fact
moment by moment. Your future and the realization of
your final goal depend upon it.

How can we gain the proper perspective on our-
selves?

You must alter your perspective to see your life and the
lives of others as part of a continuing process. This will
make life more understandable to you. Since everything
you have been and can be — your potential — exists in

the present, the barriers of time and space are no longer relevant, provided you live in the present, the eternal now.

How do we do that?

By freeing yourself from the pressures that surround you. You must function in the time and place in which you find yourself, but you must never allow yourself to become parochial in your thinking. Remember, you have experienced life in different times and countries, as different races and as both sexes, and you have been a citizen of the unseen as well as the seen world. You are a free soul who has had innumerable relationships as well as a primary relationship.

What is our primary relationship?

All other relationships fall in place when your relationship with your eternal self becomes a functioning reality. Your temporal self is to be ruled by and be one with your eternal self. The way this relationship works is through your heart feelings and the use of your spiritual equipment — your love, your sense of truth, and your intuition.

How do we activate this relationship?

Love is the only emotion that is of God, so as you express it you are aligning yourself with God in you.

The sense of truth is the infallible essence of God in you, and when you are aligned with it you are relating to your eternal self.

Intuition is the mind of the eternal self. When it is used to settle all moral and spiritual problems, the eternal self (God in you) is ruling your life.

To be related, to have relationships, what exactly does that mean?

It means you are part of, you belong to, the Whole-God. However, in your day-to-day life on earth, the Whole is reduced until it becomes something for which you can be responsible — your loved ones. Within that group there will be those to whom you particularly relate —those of your goal. But you are responsible for all of the others as well. The more you relate to God in you (your higher self), the more you bring harmony to all of your relationships, eliminating your karma in the process.

Reassembly

What would relationships be like in the discarnate world when I am no longer the me that I knew, and those to whom I am to relate are no longer recognizable as those whom I have known as wife, parent, child, or even male or female?

In the Place of Preparation you will see yourself and others much more clearly than you do now. Beginning with the aura (the center of your focus) and including the entire entity, you see one another truly as you are, although the degree of clarity does depend upon your own degree of development. When you see one another you do not see the persona — the part you played in your last incarnation — but the real self. You now relate to others as life forces, united by a common experience. You have in the past played different roles together (and will in the future), but now your job is to learn, to study the text of all your lives, your progressions and regressions, and to reassemble these elements in order to accomplish your most needed objective as you see it. You understand your unique individuality (God's Will for you) and the goal for which you were created.

Please tell me more about relating to others as life forces united by a common experience.

At this point, if you are able, it is possible to understand the true nature of life. Each entity is recognized as a unique individual life force, destined to become an indispensable element of the life force of the Whole-God. Individuality is understood as an essential element of each life force. Personality is no longer a necessary ingredient. The personas you have assumed during your innumerable incarnations no longer have validity. Individuality and uniqueness are your treasured possessions. They have been yours from the beginning, but assume their rightful position in your consciousness at this stage of the learning cycle. Your conscience and your character, the other two essential elements of your being, are earned along the way, but your individuality and uniqueness are ever with you as elements of the life force — you.

Don't our individuality and uniqueness grow also?
Your conscience and character contribute to the development of your individuality. Your uniqueness is yours from the beginning.

Will you please define individuality and uniqueness for me? I'm not clear about their differences.
The quality that distinguishes you from all others is your individuality. Your uniqueness is that about you which cannot be equalled by any other, that which is matchless.

What is the effect of this clarity of vision?
There is no sham or hypocrisy in the Place of Preparation. Things are exactly as they seem. You are what you are. You accept your limitations as a child does. As the child grows, develops, and learns year by year, so do you incarnation by incarnation. At the end of each you reassess, reassemble, and start again.

I would think that if a loved one was brighter, more luminous than I, I would feel insecure, ashamed, even jealous.

On the contrary. Your loved one's luminosity would fill you with reassurance because it would emanate love and empathy and you would feel happy to be the recipient.

Doesn't this condition tend to alter relationships?

Because all of you are seeking the same objective — to see yourself truly and move on — it is important to know your exact state of development. You understand and feel gratified to learn that the others who are more developed will be of help to you. Whatever denotes negativism is not regarded with criticism or derision, but rather with sympathy as a means of understanding one another. You recognize the condition simply as a state of growth.

Just how are we able to see ourselves?

You see yourself through your new discarnate faculties. You are able to step aside and look at yourself — who you really are as a result of who you have been.

Development is indicated to a large degree by color. The ultimate goal for all is the brilliance of clear light. However, just as brilliant clear light is comprised of all the colors of the rainbow (as seen by sunlight striking a prism), so is the potential of your ultimate brilliance and clarity comprised of all colors. In the process of your development you run the gamut of all of the colors of the rainbow, from dark to light. It has been your response to your relationships on earth that determines your color at first.

Is lightness or darkness the only indication of development?

Although one could say that the dark or light color of an individual indicates a stage of development, there are other factors that have importance too. The beauty, the glow, the clarity of any particular color says much for the quality of the development of that soul. Color is related to experience, old souls — those with more experience — generally having a lighter color than new souls. But a beautifully glowing amethyst-colored entity, although a younger soul, is clearly more constructive, having benefited more from experience than a lighter-colored entity who, although an older soul, is afflicted with dull imperfections of past deterrence, a sign of unresolved relationships. Here nothing can be concealed, good or bad.

Can we really be glad to know our lack of development?

You are glad to know the truth so you can plan your next steps toward development. You see yourself and you are comparing yourself with others.

But when you say we don't always accept the truth, are you saying that there are some who are unhappy to know their own state of development?

I am saying that there are some who don't accept all of the requirements for preparing properly for the next incarnation.

Seeing in this way must cause a difficult adjustment.

Nevertheless, readjusting your sights to let this all come into focus is your first big job in the Place of Preparation.

It requires a willingness to accept conditions as they are. You have already accepted your life review. Now, in looking back at your last incarnate life you must also be willing to understand and accept the others who are still there as they truly are. Strangely, this is often more difficult because those in the incarnate world still appear as they were when you too were incarnate. They have not yet been transformed by the process of self-judgment, so it is only through the utmost effort that you can learn to penetrate their facade and see them as they truly are.

From the Place of Preparation are we really able to see our incarnate relationships in their reactions to daily events? Wouldn't there be a frequency problem?

I'm not speaking of looking at them in their daily lives. I am saying that you must try to see them for who they now are stemming from what you have learned about their reactions to your relationships in previous incarnations you have shared. Through this effort you can learn more about them than they know about themselves. You realize that your memory of them and their actuality are quite different. It becomes difficult to put the two together, but with concentration you learn to understand their true nature.

What about my feelings about myself?

The one you left behind was a person, a personality. Without that personality you might well feel that you would not be you, that you would be someone else. However, the opposite is true because you are now the essence of what you are, devoid of all karmic, ethnic, family, earthly influences. Because of this your individuality, your uniqueness, your conscience and your character are much more clearly discernible. Your sense of yourself as well as others is immediate.

Even though your individuality and uniqueness have been yours from the beginning, and you must earn your conscience and your character during your various incarnate lives, these four essentials of your being are continually evolving, are in a continual state of becoming. Evolution is an ingredient of life itself. You not only know this in the Place of Preparation, you feel it. There is a sense of urgency in the very atmosphere of this place. You long to get on with your development toward your ultimate goal, which you now understand clearly.

This all sounds too good to be true.

For many this turns out to be the case. The life review follows immediately after death.

If you remember, in discussing evil[1] you learned that all souls are confronted with their past life and asked to see themselves as they truly are and accept what they see. Those who are unwilling and unable to do this are automatically in the frequency of the Place of Self-Deception. Those who are willing and able are automatically in the frequency of the Place of Preparation. The acceptance of truth has raised their frequency. In order to understand their last incarnation fully they are now presented with all of their previous lives. It is on the basis of that information, after it has been fully absorbed, that they prepare the conditions leading to their next incarnation. They are involved with this for the duration of their stay. Help is available to enable them to do this wisely.

---

[1] See *The Challenge of Evil* (Destiny Books, Rochester, VT, 1988).

Preparation

In view of the careful preparation you've described, why do so many of us come so ill-prepared?

The fault lies in the emotional condition of those who are going through this experience. Some become so determined to right a wrong they have done someone on earth that they decide they must return immediately while the one they have wronged is still incarnate, even though the relationship would be of a different generation.

Or they may be so affected by the grief of the one who is left behind that they decide to return. For this reason excessive grief or compulsive preoccupation with the "dead" by incarnates can seriously interfere with the progress of the discarnate one, even to the extent that the soul becomes bound to the earth frequency out of a need to stay close to the bereaved. This impedes the progress of the discarnate one needlessly. It is important for incarnates to let their loved ones go, in the hope that the relationship will be resumed only when it can be done constructively.

Is everyone affected positively by the sense of urgency that exists in the Place of Preparation?

Not necessarily. There are those at the opposite extreme who are so comfortable with the conditions they find in the Place of Preparation — the beauty, the harmony, and the fund of knowledge that exists there — that they drift into becoming perpetual students, wayfarers in the land they recall as home. They avoid the need to reincarnate, preferring instead to enjoy their homeland. They let opportunities slip by until finally after much prodding they make the move only when it seems easy. By that time they have so immunized themselves from the atmosphere of urgency that dominates the Place of Preparation that their resolve is weak. They are reluctant to return to incarnate life. As a consequence, once they do reincarnate, they are unable to relate and so they succumb to fear, giving free rein to those karmic problems with which they are now ill-prepared to cope.

What is the basis behind success or failure in reincarnating?

In considering why incarnations succeed or fail, you must not lose sight of the fact that you enter a new incarnation with the same character you had when you left the last one. The Place of Preparation is not for building character. It is a time for appraising, learning, and restructuring with whatever strengths you already have, in the expectation that the added strengths will contribute to your character during your next sojourn on earth.

You are able to do so because you are free of temptations, compulsions, karmic faults, misfortunes, and deterrent relationships — all those things that impeded your progress on earth. When the opportunities offered in the Place of Preparation are understood and fully realized, an incarnation never fails. Spiritual progress will be made no matter how difficult the karma to be overcome may be.

It is often puzzling to see that some people appear so cheerful under extreme adversity.

Many things that are puzzling in incarnate life are traceable to proper preparation. Why do some with overwhelming handicaps have such buoyant spirits and live such constructive lives with lasting, loving relationships, while others in more favorable circumstances are easily defeated, resulting in deterrent relationships? You cannot hope to understand your own life, much less the lives of others, unless you understand intuitively why you came, why you chose the family and circumstances of your life, as well as your karma, good or ill.

I find it difficult to relate the no-win situation into which some are born combining their own inadequacies and adverse relationships with the careful preparation in the Place of Preparation.

What the Place of Preparation is all about is perceiving the truth. Even when you see things as they are, you don't always embrace them. You must learn to understand God's Will versus self-will, the dangers of deterrence, the law of cause and effect, the way that you relate to the Whole through others, before you can make the right decisions concerning your next incarnation. This is not an intelligence test, it is a growing process.

If we have to perceive the truth in order to be in the Place of Preparation, how is it that we have allowed the balance of power on earth to shift to the side of deterrence and evil?[1]

Even though you may see yourself clearly, if your perception of any one of the elements that go into a successful incarnation should falter, the outcome would result in some form of deterrence instead of construction. However, when an incarnation seems to have failed before it really has begun, it may not be a failure of

---

[1] See *The Challenge of Evil* (Destiny Books, Rochester, VT, 1988).

perception, but a deliberate self-sacrifice. It is important to try to see and accept the whole picture and not
make judgments.

What is it we learn from studying our past lives?

As you study your past lives you will see them with
more objectivity than you had during your life review.
The first thing you will learn is your goal; the final goal
for which you were created. I say learn, but it is more a
matter of realization. You will feel yourself a part of those
whose goal is the same as yours. This becomes a source
of joy and love, a sense of well being and happiness, just
to be together.

From what source do we study our past lives?

Your lives are recorded. Information about your entire
existence is available. You can learn about all of your
lives from the beginning of the granting of free will. From
this you are able to peruse the circumstances of your various relationships, seeing just who they were and the
part they played during your multifarious incarnations,
right up to who you are now.

Are we also able to see the relative importance of our various relationships?

Yes. You must learn to see the importance of some relationships over others because this knowledge is essential in setting about to choose your next set of parents,
even though that decision would usually come only after
much self-development.

Could we say that each incarnation has a purpose?

Each incarnation is an opportunity, a chance to add to
your character a quality that will advance you spiritually. In the Place of Preparation you conceive and then

work to acquire the essence of a quality you know you need to move forward. In the incarnate world your job is to develop it in quantity by living it out, thus making it a permanent element of your character. You will decide what quality to develop this time on the basis of how well you succeeded last time. Whether it be courage, honesty, humility, energy, objectivity, patience, benevolence — whatever — it will be an important factor in your future decisions.

How do we identify our karma?

Your karma is your own legacy. It is what you have created for yourself, good or ill. It affects everything about you. You cannot escape it. It demands action. Your job in the Place of Preparation is to see and recognize it as a result of studying the records of your past lives, to understand it and to prepare to cope with it in the incarnate world the next time around. It is because of the inescapable inevitability of coping with karma on earth that self-examination and realization (a private response to one's own conscience) can have such profound results. To recognize what you are doing while you are still incarnate, to acknowledge it, and make amends can free you from the karmic consequences that would otherwise result.

What do you mean by karmic consequences?

What you are is the result of what you have been and done. In the incarnate experience you get what you have earned. What harm you have caused others will be experienced in like degree by you ultimately alleviating the resultant deterrence.

Recognition of this fact and the realization that you have chosen to cope with it create a constructive attitude. If you act on this attitude by accepting consequent circumstances in true humility, it will result in overcoming some of your karmic problems, and your next incarnation can be built on new strength. You understand that the more construction you can engender now in your relationships, the less deterrence will carry over into your future relationships with less difficulties to overcome. You realize that it is you who will have to live the future you are creating now. The law of cause and effect is inescapable.

What is the nature of deterrent relationships?

Deterrent relationships are inevitably karmic. They reveal a spiritual need that has not been resolved, and one that you by yourself may or may not be able to resolve in your present incarnation. However, it is important to understand that it is crucial to try to make every effort to alleviate all possible problems. The longer karmic difficulties in relationships remain unresolved, the more complicated it becomes to overcome them. This could take many incarnations to accomplish.

Are abnormalities given us because of some past prideful acts on our part for instance, or are we to think, as we have thought, that they are given us to advance us spiritually by teaching us humility? I realize that both causes could result in the same effect — humility — but the one seems automatic and cold while the other seems loving and caring. Please help me understand this.

You want to feel that someone cares and has given you this out of love in the hope that it will bring you to clear vision. Please understand that moral law stems from the Love of God. If we were not important to God, the law wouldn't exist. Moral law is the means through which we are allowed over and over to examine behavior and consequences. It is intended as a guidepost. If you flaunt yourself in the face of the law, you suffer the consequences. That's that.

Aside from being the result of the law of cause and effect, does a disfigurement serve any other purpose, since the person who has it can't possibly know why?

The purpose is to teach a lesson — to accept all that comes to you as your due. You always get what you need, and in this case you need to be reminded of past wrongs (some of which you may recognize as your present unresolved faults) so you can strive to lead a more constructive life recognizing the need for humility.

I should think that that would be very hard to do if one is emotionally involved with hating the hurtful comments of others, however unintentional. It's a lot to expect from a child.

Surely a child suffers greatly from past wrongs. However, through the suffering much can be gained and, finally, if the lesson (humility) is learned, one's spiritual development, one's frequency, is raised.

But what about great suffering in an incarnation as a choice?

This is a decision to move forward more quickly by alleviating past wrongs in a massive effort to respond constructively to all events against enormous odds. A decision to expedite matters in this way can be made, but just what one is given is not known.

Are physical limitations always karmic?

Yes.

Is what we get always related to what we have done?

Yes.

Then when we decide to reincarnate, do we know if we deserve a karmic albatross — that we may have earned it?

Yes, you recognize that you deserve it, but you don't know just what it might be.

Why not?

Because it is determined by your ledger, your debits and credits, in what categories they fall. The actual result comes from the working out of moral law.

Is there no compassion?

It is not a question of judgment, but of mathematics so to speak. You have done it to yourself. You are given exactly what you deserve. The law is the law. God is not mocked.

So whatever is brought about is the result of past incarnate relationships?

All movement, either up or down the frequency scale, is determined by relationships.

Is it also true that benefits must be earned in accordance with moral law?

All good that comes to you is yours by right. You have earned it.

And this is true of ill also?

Yes.

But isn't whether something is good or ill dependent on interpretation?

You are correct. You could accept what appears to be ill as something good, a lesson to be learned, and therefore desirable, making it good.

Then nothing need ever be ill?

This attitude is part of development. It takes an advanced soul to turn ill to good.

Is the help we receive from your side personal or somehow automatic?

If you pray to your discarnate loved ones for help in your efforts, you will receive help in accordance with need. If you pray for them and they for you, the help engendered is reciprocal. Or say you have a need for God's Love and you pray for help to overcome a problem that you feel you can't handle alone. The response to that need is met in proportion to the validity of the intention in asking and the need God has for you, freed of deterrence.

What exactly do you mean by that?

Your own development plays a part in the response to need. If you have developed to the degree that you are prepared to become a servant of God, your need will express this development and it will be met accordingly. If you are a new soul and your needs are basic, the response will reflect this.

Are you saying the more developed soul has earned a different response to need than the less developed soul?

I'm saying that the degree of spiritual development is responded to in like degree.

How is that determined?
Through the Law of Parallels.

I understand the Law of Parallels when it concerns constructive and deterrent thoughts and acts,[1] but when it is a plea for help I can't see what the parallel response would be. If a need is expressed, what do you get? Oh, I see...
...Yes, of course you see. You get what you need. Remember, you'd better want what you need because what you need is what you'll get. If what you want is deterrent, then what you need is to learn that lesson. What you get will teach you the error of your ways. This you learned in some of our early conversations.[2]

So this too must be an automatic working out of moral law?
Yes indeed.

Is karma involved with the circumstances of our lives?
This situation is often misconstrued. Fortunate circumstances are not necessarily a manifestation of good karma, nor unfortunate of bad karma. Seeming difficulties and apparent tragedies may be growth opportunities you have come to realize, whereas wealth, talent, etc., may represent challenging problems that you must generate the energy and the discipline to cope with constructively in accordance with God's Will for you. In any case, it is the way you react to the circumstances of your life that determines its outcome.

---

[1] See *The Challenge of Evil* (Destiny Books, Rochester, VT, 1985).
[2] See *Why You Are Who You Are* (Destiny Books, Rochester, VT, 1988).

What determines how I react?

How well you react to the circumstances of your life depends upon your attitude toward life itself — whether or not it seems good. How well you reassemble in the Place of Preparation is dependent largely on your character — that which you are and that which you will become by adding the qualities you develop each incarnation and by living them out in the incarnate state.

What happens to those I've harmed if I don't do restitution until a later incarnation?

Whenever and wherever you make restitution for the harm you have done, you release the other person as well as yourself from the negative karma that has bound you together. To understand this, you must come to realize that when you harm another it is God you are harming. Your fundamental relationship is with God. If you harm anyone or anything you are harming God as well. Through the mystical transference of God's Love, the one injured will be released from any karmic residue resulting from your negative actions once you have made restitution. When your paths cross again, your relationship will be constructive.

Focus

What happens right after death?

Shortly after physical death you find yourself drawn into the presence of God. This you experience in proportion to your own receptivity. The review of your life with which you are confronted at this time is illumined by the presence of God, enabling you to face it honestly unless you are blinded by self-deception.

To be drawn into the presence of God in proportion to our own receptivity — what exactly does that imply?

Your perception of the significance of the event, the extent of the radiance of the Being before you, the sensations you experience, and the result of the encounter depend in large measure on your receptivity resulting from your spiritual preparedness.

You say the radiant figure is God. Could you be more specific?

Remember that God works through people. The radiant figure is a perfectly developed servant of God, a holy one who is serving God's Will in this way — a manifestation of God.

Are we drawn into the Presence first of all?

Yes.

Even if our expectations are nil?

Most souls don't know what to expect. What is important is your recognition of the reality before you. The
development of your character and conscience plays a
large part in your reception of the truth you face at this
point.

*Could there be some who might arrive there but
would be unable to relate?*

Yes, this is possible. Those who have led nondeterrent
lives but who have gained little or nothing from the experience, due to lack of concentration and energy, will find
themselves unable to perceive the significance of the
review, and the Presence will be only dimly realized.

What happens to such souls?

They are taken in hand by their Guardians and are given
healing, energizing treatment until they are prepared to
go through the experience once again. There are more
examples of this kind than you can imagine.

*I understand that we are often met by friends and
loved ones. When does this take place?*

Even though some advanced souls pass directly into
the Place of Preparation, for most it is only after they
have passed the initial tests. Once the Place of Preparation is gained, every effort is made to make you feel
at home and comfortable with those you know and love.
Recognizing your Guardian is a great boon to your feeling of well being.

*I can imagine that if, all unbeknown to some, they
are suddenly confronted by a radiant, brilliant
Presence that must be almost blinding to behold,
showing them what they have done with their lives*

— the sham, the shame, the lies and deceptions, as well as any efforts towards harmony and construction — that they could, as a result, experience frightening insecurity. Am I right?

Your thoughts have merit, but are limited. The reactions of many affect the fundamental elements of the soul. Latent insecurity brings on fear and even terror, rendering the spiritual equipment powerless, resulting in disintegration. However, the Guardian is always at hand prepared to do what is necessary to integrate the soul in an effort to see clearly at last. This could be a prolonged effort, but Guardians are dedicated to growth and development and therefore are willing to do what is necessary to alleviate any and all negative conditions.

What exactly disintegrates?

As the result of incipient fear, character and conscience lose their function, individuality and uniqueness become scattered. Total disintegration follows. This is an outcome of ignoring preparation and little or no growth.

Our Guardian Angels are obviously crucial to the plan of our lives.

Once you arrive in the Place of Preparation, your Guardian becomes not only your primary relationship but also, you realize, your oldest relationship. Because the Guardians have stayed in the discarnate world abiding by the Will of God, they are angelic souls with a limited knowledge of evil. Their job is to guard and help those who have made the dangerous choice.

How can they guard if they don't know about evil?

It isn't that they don't know, they don't experience evil. Evil has no power over them, as evil must gain entry through self-will, the outcome of free will. Although the will of all Guardians is tied to the Will of God, God does not interfere with your free will. That is a covenant with you.

Just how do our Guardians serve us?

They are both inner and outer realities, existing in the unseen world in angelic form, and also in the seen world through your consciousness. They are intermediaries between your discarnate and your incarnate selves. They function through your spiritual equipment, influencing you by appealing to your love, sense of truth, and intuition, whether you are discarnate or incarnate. When you are in the Place of Preparation they are made manifest to you. They are your teachers and advisors, your protectors and your friends. You can now see objectively and understand what was subjective when you were on earth.

Some of us have spirit guides with whom we communicate. Could you in fact be my Guardian Angel?

Spirit guides are not angels. They are discarnates who have experienced but no longer need the reincarnation cycle. The two have very different functions. A spirit guide communicates to achieve a task that can only be accomplished through communication — such a task as we are undertaking. When an incarnate is receptive and prepared, a spirit guide will attempt to cultivate the opportunity to impart an aspect of truth to the incarnate world through communication. This discarnate – incarnate psychic interplay takes on many forms, depending upon the particular talent of the incarnate. It may start on a personal level, but if, after a period of trial, it remains concentrated on the personal, if the incarnate continues to be interested only in trivia or if it is used for individual advantage, the contact will gradually lose energy and fall into confusion. Your Guardian Angel will try to alert you to the dangers of Deterrent Force that contribute to this, but may not succeed.

Since Deterrent Force doesn't exist in the Place of Preparation, what do Guardian Angels guard against?

Deterrent Force[1] doesn't exist, but your own thoughts and feelings can still be deterrent. You can deter your own progress through your reactions to circumstances. For instance, your Guardian will guide you through the dangers inherent in reviewing your past lives — to see those lives objectively and to understand their relevance to you as you now are. Your reactions to this process could affect you negatively. Remember that those who are seeking to reincarnate are still imperfect — they have much to eliminate and much to add.

Grasping the differences that exist in the two worlds must be overwhelming at first.

The more you learn in the Place of Preparation, the more you are made aware of the differences that exist in relation to earth life. As an example, your perception of time, space, and motion will alter. You come to realize that they are all one concept in the discarnate world. They cannot be separated. They all become elements of the moment and are realized simultaneously. Within a thought lies its realization. For example, your desire to be elsewhere puts you there instantly. However, your ability to perceive and understand all of the various functions of the discarnate world is dependent upon your particular degree of development — your frequency

---

[1] See *The Challenge of Evil* (Destiny Books, Rochester, VT, 1988).

level. You are able to gain an understanding of how the use of free will on earth affects life in the discarnate world if your level of frequency warrants it. The review of the relationships within your former lives will include both the incarnate and discarnate aspects of those lives.

What is gained from seeing our past incarnate lives?

You learn just how fully you accepted yourself in the past, how you related to the problems and needs within your relationships, as well as how well you prepared to cope with what you believed to be your present problems each time. You see how long it took you to come to grips with your problems each time, resisting the beauty that surrounded you, and finally making the decision to incarnate again and subject yourself once more to that great unknown adventure. You are thus made aware of the importance of proper preparation and the inevitable result of the lack of it. The law of cause and effect is now a reality. This becomes still another facet of what has been a very sobering and humbling experience. You resolve to do it right this time. However, a certain trepidation often accompanies this decision.

If we see ourselves and others in the Place of Preparation, are we also able to see those in the other regions?

You are able to see those who are in the Place of Self-Deception as they truly are as well as the person they imagine themselves to be. You focus on those with whom you have had relationships, and if you recognize loved ones among them it could cause you great pain. Even though you might empathize with their problems, you would nevertheless find yourself helpless to do anything about their plight. However, if after lengthy preparation and diligent effort on your own problems you are able to raise your frequency sufficiently, this could enable you to cope with the negativity of your loved ones and help them to see the error in which they are enmeshed. If you persist in your efforts to help, you may be able to turn them toward the light of truth. This could justify a prolonged stay in the Place of Preparation.

I thought it took a very developed soul to help those in the Place of Self-Deception. Is it possible for an ordinary struggling soul to do this?

Yes it is. It becomes a matter of frequency. If you are able to raise your frequency sufficiently to gain the tensile strength to overcome the negative stress to which you would be subjected, you could be a positive influence with your shared love as a guiding light.

Can we see those in the Lower Regions too?

Although you are able to perceive the Lower Regions from where you are, you are unable to relate to those who are there. Only those in the Higher Realms can administer help without violating the integrity of their spirits.

What about those in the Higher Realms? Do we see them?

Those from the First Realm are teachers in the Place of Preparation. This becomes an element of their development. Those from the Higher Realms visit the Place of Preparation frequently, and also those in the Place of Preparation who have raised their frequency sufficiently are able to gain glimpses of the Higher Realms just as some on earth have been able to glimpse the higher frequency of the Place of Preparation.

When we set out to reassemble, what is our primary consideration?

Relationships are the primary consideration of all those in the Place of Preparation. The qualities they gain and the subsequent character that develops in the incarnate world will depend upon their relationships and what they do about them. To understand their objective and develop in accordance with God's Will they must be able to grasp the nature of the process of reincarnation —why they don't just go on developing as the same people.

Isn't it the family concept that tends to hold people together?

It is true that when you think of relationships you think of family. But now you are required to readjust your thinking. Although the family structure is continuous, your part in that structure varies. The thought that you could be your child's child, for instance, demands a 180-degree turnaround in your thinking. What does this mean? It means that you relate to one another as elements of God, and as elements of God you fulfill any role that serves a purpose toward your ultimate relationship with God. Along the way you play many parts. Depending upon the faculties you need to develop and the way you need to relate to one another, you become many different personalities. Now try to extend that thought to all of life and every time and place.

How do we play those various parts? Who assigns the roles?

Remember, the play is continuous. The earth is the stage and the Place of Preparation is backstage. Backstage the makeup and the props are gone. The actors are themselves. They recall the roles they have played in the past and they anticipate the next role they are to play. They

consider the qualities they will need to develop to fulfill
their next role and they dream of the perfect cast — how,
why, and with whom they want to act and react.

In the Place of Preparation any relationship can be
brought into focus in accordance with need. Knowledge
of any and all your relationships is possible, but if it isn't
relevant to the need of the moment it won't focus for long.
Out of need, relationships tend to converge, creating an
inner urgency that is acted on when the time comes for
you to select your parents and prepare to make an
entrance on stage.

On stage you exist on two levels. You are the part you
are playing this time, and you are also yourself (the eternal you). So now when you relate to others and they
relate to you in the present drama, it is on two levels
whether or not this is a conscious fact.

Where does the text for this drama originate?

It comes from the interaction of human beings. It exists,
it is ongoing and continuous. You enter the drama choosing the moment when you can interact with someone
with whom you want to relate. The story line for you
exists only in potential. Although your character has
been preconceived, it is actually developed in the process of playing this particular role. When you make your
entrance (are born) the drama is in progress. The stage
is set, the actors present, the emotional dynamics exist,
and a probable story will unfold — probable, but not
inevitable. That depends on you and all the others on
stage. The force of the action, the strength of intention,
and the quality of the playing may bring about a change
in the script. Improvisation could bring out hidden
meaning. An actor may forget his part or commit a
sudden irrational act, or he may dominate the plot for
good or for ill, so that the meaning of the play, even the

preconceived story line, is altered. However, because of
the relationships that are present in this particular act
of the drama, a strong sense of probability exists even
though, with the unpredictability of human behavior,
anything is possible. You come to realize that if you give
yourself to each scene of the play moment by moment,
you will end up having fulfilled the purpose of the play
and satisfied the Author's dream, becoming a truly functioning member of the cast.

Opportunity

Are you saying that if we play our parts right, realizing each moment, that no matter how complicated the scene it will always turn out as the Author wants it?

I'm saying that each incarnation (play) is an opportunity, and that the greatest benefit resulting from the understanding of that fact is the effect it has on you. To realize that now — any present moment, whatever it is — is an opportunity, can have a freeing effect on you. You find yourself released from your tensions and negations, seeing what is positive in it. It is a great gift of God's Grace that negative-seeming aspects of life can be as much opportunities as positive ones.

What kinds of opportunities are we faced with?

They are opportunities to use your spiritual equipment, to develop your character and your conscience, thus contributing to your individuality, to cultivate the quality you came to develop in quantity in order to repay a karmic debt and develop your relationships in the context of the particular circumstances in which you find yourself. Bearing in mind that you gained those circumstances out of your choice of parents, you realize that no matter how difficult they may seem they must be purposeful.

How can we make use of these various opportunities?

By consciously allowing your sense of truth, which

is ever with you, to rise to the surface, you are able to see things as they truly are, not as they seem to be. You see the value of this experience to you and your development and just how you have contributed to the situation yourself. Stop trying to justify your problems, but trust the way this realization makes you feel about them now instead. You are thereby permitting the mind of your discarnate self — your intuition — to control your life in accordance with God's Will for you. Your love, the element of God in you, becomes the conduit through which you give voice to your feelings, elevating them to a spiritual level.

Through this use of your spiritual equipment your character and conscience grow, contributing to the qualities that signal the development of your individuality. All of this affects your relationships for the better, allowing you to function within the circumstances of your life constructively.

Is there further development?

The moment you seek and discover the opportunity embedded in all circumstances you will have learned to use negation to create construction — the mark of a developed soul. Pain becomes courage, ennui becomes energy, discord becomes harmony.

In this way you learn who you really are. Before you reincarnated you had, with consideration and advice, conceived of the plan of your next incarnate life whole, but once you have actually reincarnated you must achieve that whole, moment by moment.

Are we actually involved in the plan of our lives each time?

The plan of your life is drawn up each time by you and

your advisors. The choice of the parental circumstances that would best bring this about is up to you.

Why aren't we conscious of that original concept once we are here?

You are conscious of it intuitively. It becomes what you really want, your most fundamental longing, your ideal. Even though many people lose sight of this fundamental longing, the potential, at a deep level, is always there.

If you were aware of the original conception of your potential you would become rigid, trying to make all circumstances fit the concept instead of coping with life as it is. This would deprive you of the spontaneous creativity that enables you to meet the unexpected. You would react intellectually instead of utilizing your intuition and the other elements of your spiritual equipment. The opportunity inherent in incarnate life is granted to you moment by moment, so that is the way to respond. As you ask yourself what the opportunity of this moment offers and you find the answer to that question, you will feel life opening before you.

The moment is comprised of two parts: the offer and your response to it. One is always in proportion to the other. A passing moment responded to either negatively or positively has little lasting effect, whereas the response to a complex or profound moment may alter a whole life as well as lives to come.

What effect does this have on our future?

It affects the very core of your life. You are creating your own legacy. Think about that. Think about your close relationships, realizing that the particular way that you relate to others is a one-time opportunity. That should be a sobering thought. You will relate to them over and over but in different ways, never again like this. And if your thoughts about them are negative, reparations will have to be made sooner or later.

I think that it is easier to imagine living in different times and places than to imagine switching gender or parent – child relationships.

This is because your present relationships are so personal to you and because you need to concentrate on your present role. You must simply take for granted that experiencing both genders as well as relating to those you love in varying ways is an enriching, beneficial experience intimately tied to your innermost being. Relationships are the core of life. If you consider the many aspects of love you will realize you cannot experience them all in one lifetime, but you can and will over many lifetimes. Every opportunity for you to express love is an opportunity for you to become the Love of God on earth.

It occurs to me that this is what our myths and legends dramatize for us.

Myths and legends show us how far we can rise and how far we can fall. They are humanity's view of the adventures and opportunities of life as they appear in the furthest intuitive reaches of imagination. We see what it means to be transformed by good or evil, and we see that this takes place through the mystical intermingling of the Seen and the Unseen.

It's hard to see that there must be untold millions of us somewhere in another dimension doing something.

If you believe in immortality, you must realize that every soul ever created has to be somewhere right now. Imagination and intuition are opportunities. They open the door to symbolic truth.

Absorption

Although relationships must be important, they often seem pointless and annoying.

There is no relationship that is pointless. All relationships have some meaning, even the most annoying, especially the most annoying, because this indicates that the relationship needs mending. Or it may be a situation upon which no true relationship can be based. If you have allowed yourself to become involved in a circumstance that seems pointless and troublesome this is because you have allowed yourself to wander too far from your source. To understand why you feel this way you must find your way back to that source — God. You are best able to see things clearly if your vision is livened by the knowledge that you are a part of the Whole. The life that courses through you courses through all, even those who annoy you or those whom you don't like. You didn't start this life flow and you can't stop it. It is that vital flow that has enlivened you from the beginning, not only physically but also spiritually.

Please explain the spiritual aspects of this.

You are sustained physically. You breathe in and you breathe out. Similarly, you are sustained spiritually by what you take in and what you give out. If two people are compatible they are able to function together and think as one. This takes place through the process of absorption. In this situation you are constantly absorbing each other's thoughts, emotions, values, aspirations, insecurities, securities, likes, and dislikes. Your thoughts and feelings mesh. The construction in you is absorbed by others and so is the deterrence. In this way whole groups of people can become creative or constricted.

Surely we don't absorb in this way from everyone we know?

No. Certainly not. There are three basic avenues of absorption — relationships of blood, of goal, and of course of love. When love accompanies the other two situations, the tendency toward harmonious absorption is far greater. There are also other conditions in which absorption takes place. The weak can absorb from the strong, the insecure from the deterrent and evil, groups from espoused ideology of charismatic figures of any and all persuasions. Much of absorption is achieved through emotion. Negativity emanating from one person can be absorbed by those within the environment who are susceptible. In this way whole societies can absorb the tenets of a few persuasive fanatics.

Doesn't this depend upon the nature of the society?

It is true that the process of absorption is influenced by the structure of the society. The great value of a democracy is that people are free to absorb many different kinds of influences. The difficulty, however, of a materialistic-oriented democracy is that it provides opportunity for access channels to be so manipulated and controlled that people as a whole tend to absorb the values of a few.

Also, the scientific age has enormously increased the ability of the aggressive to dominate for profit. Nevertheless, even this is still infinitely preferable to a dictatorship, where it is fear that is absorbed, preventing freedom from functioning, particularly freedom of religion, freedom of the family to worship.

How does fear affect absorption?

Through fear one is rendered helpless to be and act in accordance with one's sense of truth and intuition. This victimizes the spirit and prevents clear thinking. What one is absorbing is insecurity stemming from the atmosphere created by cruel punishment of the innocent by fanatic rulers for ideological reasons.

Not knowing what to expect next paralyzes one's normal responses, allowing absorbed insecurity and fear to rule one's nature.

Does the family have a special concern here?

It smacks of piety to say that God functions through the family, but let's think about this for a moment. You realize that parental love is not something you learn. It is in you and part of you. It is absorbed from God. It is the God in you nurturing those who are venturing into a new incarnate life. There are unfortunately some who neither want nor love their children. They have the capacity to do so but are prevented by powerful karmic problems.

Parental love, or hate, is absorbed by the children, whether or not they are aware of it, because children are spiritually porous. They absorb easily. What they absorb from you as parents will eventually be given out and absorbed by others. The responsibility of your love for your children cannot be overestimated. The adults your children become will in part be you. Think of this.

You mentioned love as an element of absorption. Please clarify.

When normal feelings of love accompany sexual attraction resulting in fulfillment, God is functioning. If you are not sensitive to this feeling, if you don't believe in it, you separate sex from genuine sharing and in this respect you will not only be failing to absorb the love of your partner but also the Love of God. But if you truly love your sexual partner, you will not only be absorbing but also giving God's Love.

Are there limits to absorption?

Even under ideal conditions, the process of absorption is conditioned and limited by predisposition. The character with which you come and the karmic aspects of your relationships necessarily make you more or less predisposed to absorb either good or ill, and even evil, from others.

Are you saying that our absorption is related to our own condition rather than that of others?

Yes, exactly. A person who is well prepared to live out the qualities developed to eliminate weaknesses will in no way absorb deterrence or evil from others because of the strength of purpose that results. Lack of preparation, however, leads to absorption of deterrence of all kinds, from simple negativism to evil. If you had a need to mend a former relationship that ended with profound problems left unresolved, this need could make you vulnerable to deterrent thoughts and acts stemming from innate built-up frustration.

It's hard to think we have to cope with past problems as well as present problems.

There is no difference as far as you are concerned. Your past problems are your present problems and are therefore capable of present solutions, just as your present problems will become your future problems if left unresolved. In fact, you have actually come to deal with these various problems.

Must we continue with all relationships?

Relationships are not disposable. This is not a disposable world. All things remain in one form or another. Even thoughts are things that contribute either to the forces of good or evil. Our relationships are enduring. Our family relationships are integral, a part of ourselves. They are part of the warp and woof of our lives woven into them. Taking for granted that you once related to your present parents in a very different way since you chose them out of need, think how important it is to relate to them now constructively. If elements of negativity remain, how important it is to make them positive this time. If the relationship is positive, what a privilege to build on it and make it grow. What an opportunity you have to develop love in a new way, calling on different qualities in you to be absorbed by your loved ones!

What about relationships in which we feel little or no compatibility?

Whatever difficulties you face in your relationships it will help you to return to the least common denominator. Consider what you have in common and then focus on it. If you remain objective you will be able to broaden that base. Whatever you have in common, if looked at selflessly, will form an absorbent bond. This applies whether the relationship is one of choice — of common interest or attraction — or one that is unavoidable —family. The latter is both simpler and more difficult. It is simpler because you have no choice and it is more difficult for the same reason.

What if you just can't find a common denominator?
If the negatives become predominant you have allowed yourself to become caught up in them. Return to common ground. What is basic to your relationship? Look behind the personality to the true character. In considering character try to understand the effects of karma, the purpose in coming, the qualities that need to be developed.

How can we know these things about another person?
You know the person as someone you think you don't like. When you consider why this is so you see negative qualities in that person that are detrimental to your relationship. However, you must also recognize that your response suggests that you too have negative qualities that damage the relationship. If you realize your need to overcome these detrimental attributes, you must also accept that the other person may be trying to do likewise. You recognize that we are all here to overcome those things that contribute to discord in relationships. By seeing the good in yourself, you are able to see the good in others, recognizing that concentrating on what is good can help both you and your relationships through mutual absorption.

But haven't we been told that we can't truly know another person?
You could recognize that much that is troublesome is inevitably karmic in nature and that the person could be trying to overcome this, even though it may not appear so. In recognizing what is needed to be developed, you could find a kindred spirit under it all since you realize that you too are striving to eliminate faults and to acquire positive qualities. By seeing yourselves in the

same struggle, you could see the qualities you have in common and also the best qualities that you two very dissimilar people can absorb from each other.

Would you say that the process of absorption is largely subconscious?

Yes. It is on a subconscious level that the process of absorption pervades the family, the community, or society as a whole. Depending upon whether what you are absorbing is good or ill for you, this will raise or lower your frequency. The lowered frequency will not be altered unless awareness of what is happening is brought to the surface and dealt with.

What is the outcome of absorption?

By absorbing the good or ill around you, your own inner condition is altered so that you attract and also absorb either Constructive Force or Deterrent Force from the discarnate world. The good or ill you have absorbed is thereby activated, accelerating your movement toward and involvement in good or ill.

You have mentioned absorption regarding family relationships but, for instance, what about relationships of similar goal whom we don't know personally? Do we absorb in a like manner from them?

When something deep within you is reached and you feel yourself responding to conditions with joy and pleasure, when you are "in sync" with your surroundings, it is probably vibrations you are absorbing from someone of your own goal who has reached and expressed truth.

Could this not also be the fruition of a series of circumstances involving family or friends?

Yes, of course it could. But I would like to stress a different kind of relationship that can cause you to feel this way. What I am speaking of now is usually impersonal. It could be someone you don't know or someone who is not on earth (a composer, an author), but someone never-theless from whom you can absorb truth either directly or through the person's work. Because you recognize a kinship to that person, you are attuned to what is being said to you. This stems from having the same goal.

This is not to say that you cannot absorb good from those of all goals. Of course you can. You may love the works of many composers, for instance, but there could be one to whom you respond in a very personal way — a shock of recognition. As you absorb the quality of the talent of that person, that person (discarnate or incar-nate) absorbs your love and appreciation.

It would seem that you are now talking about the effects from the unseen world. Is there more to learn here?

It is the unseen aspects of this subject of absorption that are least understood and yet are extremely vital to the outcome of an incarnation. A person who puts self-will (deterrence) aside to do God's Will (construction) is thereby absorbing Constructive Force from the unseen world. Those who put God's Will aside to follow self-will open themselves up to absorb Deterrent Force from the unseen world. It enters the individual through fear, vanity, pride, insecurity, lack of faith, etc., and unless prevented, can take possession.

What is it that makes the difference in what one absorbs?

The difference between those who absorb good and those who absorb evil is that those who absorb good have come prepared to remain in control even though they still must make every effort to put self-will and deterrence aside in order to understand and do God's Will. But those who follow self-will isolate themselves emotionally from God's Will because emotional isolation is the nature of self-will. As a result, Deterrent Force from the unseen world rushes in and is absorbed, filling the vacuum created by this isolation, bringing on the need for gratification, for power, etc.

How is absorption manifested?

At both ends of the spectrum the process of absorption from the unseen world may become manifest in hunches, visions, voices, etc., but the effect of each is entirely different. Those who absorb Constructive Force are enormously benefited, even transformed by the process, leading to a fuller life lived in both worlds. Whereas those who absorb Deterrent Force are emotionally disturbed by their visions, their voices, and can even be compelled by them to deterrent and evil acts. Some are even possessed by them. For good or for ill, absorption from the unseen world can become the most potent force in your life.

Every thought and action of yours is responded to (paralleled) from the unseen world. The harm or benefit of your actions is responded to in kind, and you are the recipient of the effect of that paralleled action. The lift that you feel from an act of generosity generates energy, just as the sadistic exhilaration you feel from vindictiveness does. This tends to raise or lower your frequency in accordance with the positive or negative energy created.

Is there more on absorption from the unseen world?

Assistance from the unseen world — that occupies the same space as the seen world at a higher frequency level

— is at hand, available for the asking. Through the Law of Parallels you are continually reinforced in your thoughts and acts in relation and proportion to the thoughts and acts themselves. It is automatic, functioning in accordance with moral law (cause and effect). Absorption from the unseen world then is not only automatic but inevitable. It behooves you to try to keep your thoughts and acts constructive for your own sake, because if fed by your imagination they grow into something far greater than your original thought, affecting you profoundly, constructively or deterrently.

How does absorption from the unseen world affect us?

First of all, since it is through your compulsions and negativism (manifestations of karmic problems) that you absorb deterrence from the unseen world, you must try never to be misguided by them. If you know how to deal with your compulsions you eliminate deterrence that affects you negatively through absorption. Remember, you cope with compulsion by learning to sense its inception. To recognize that familiar feeling and learn to turn your attention toward construction before deterrence can get a hold of you is, of course, the answer.[1] This feat, although not simple, can be accomplished with desire power and determination and a fundamental need for construction. If, however, your thoughts and desires are both deterrent, if you have no wish to eliminate your compulsive drives, you have lost sight of your purpose in coming and the absorption from the unseen world will add drastic karmic results.

---

[1] See *Why You Are Who You Are* (Destiny Books, Rochester, VT, 1985).

Is there a principle behind absorption?

You are all spiritually porous, you absorb readily. All that constitutes your world, seen or unseen, can become a part of your being if you so desire. It is important to open yourself freely to all that is positive and constructive and to protect yourself from deterrence and evil. To do this you need to become aware of the alchemy of absorption — how one is changed by it. The most profound affect of these changes can be in individuality. The more evil you absorb, the less you are yourself. The more good you absorb, the more you are yourself — the individual you have the potential to become.

Sometimes one needs to relocate, not geographically but spiritually.

Are you saying that acts of evil can actually deprive us of our individuality?

I am saying that those who are enveloped in evil are no longer relating to their original selves, to the individuality with which they were created, because evil deprives one of individuality. All such people become much the same, without individual traits. Through the absorption of evil they become merely elements of evil with no apparent shred of individuality. This is only one of the devastating ultimate results of succumbing to and absorbing negation, deterrence, and finally evil.

Conversely then, the good we absorb from the unseen must contribute to our individuality?

Yes, you see this all around you in all of the good people as well as the great and creative people. Inspiration is a function of absorption. Those who are inspired to do what they know is theirs to do literally absorb whatever they need in proportion to their faith in themselves and their capabilities — the inner knowledge of what they are capable of accomplishing. This conviction is the very act of absorption coming from the unseen world to those who are receptive. They are living out qualities of their ultimate goal.

Who You Are

I understand about my relationships, both incarnate and discarnate, but who am I?

You are an immortal individual, a cosmos, a world in yourself. Just as your incarnate individuality is made graphic by your finger prints, so your immortal soul, of which you are not fully aware, has borne its own stamp of individuality from its inception.

Is it possible to know one's own individuality and that of others?

Only by recognizing conscience and character in addition to personality, and the effect they have on oneself and others. Individuality is determined by many things, but these three elements serve as guiding posts to understanding

What does immortality imply?

Immortality implies potential, and potential requires change. In order to bring about change while you are in the incarnate world, endless resources are available to you: energy resulting from effort, knowledge obtained through intuition, the expansion of creativity resulting from imagination, harmony proceeding from love, constructive relationships resulting from following your heart, the chance to start again — God's Grace.

Ordinarily, incarnate life is cut off from conscious memory of the past in order to be able to make a fresh start. It is not, however, cut off from the karmic faults you carry with you to remind you of your past, or from channels to the unseen. You can depend on your spiritual equipment. Your present character is the index to your former lives. You deal with your karmic heritage, both good and bad, every day of your life. Just as you have had a past that has shaped you, you also have a future that you are shaping now.

This time of your life (the incarnate state) is a time for discovery, creativity, and experimentation. You are creating a life, for good or for ill. Realizing this can open up paths of thought that can lead you away from concentration on nothing but your problems, pointing you toward a constructive path, toward growth.

What brings about spiritual growth?

The urge to grow. Life as it is to be lived on earth has an ingrained purposefulness, an impetus that must be satisfied — a goal. The urge to grow is always present, not just physically and mentally, but spiritually as well. Think what this means.

You are aware of your urge to grow, but unfortunately this is often debased as an urge to succeed as that is currently understood. Success may follow the urge to grow, but it must follow, not motivate it. If the urge to grow is stunted, malformation of some kind will result. If it is responded to positively and constructively, even human proclivities toward deterrence can be transcended and can become a conduit for God's Will on earth.

You speak of the urge to grow. Is it the same as the will to live?

The will to live is the force behind the acting out of one's need to reincarnate. Those who are clear about what they want to accomplish, strong in their desire to overcome their faults as they see them, and drawn by love to their family and other relationships, always have a strong will to live. Such people cannot be discouraged or deterred, even though they may not know why they feel the way they do. However, recognizing that the result of the urge to grow and the will to live in spite of all events can lead to a constructive life for others can help those who are hesitant and not strongly intentioned. A real effort to recognize and relate to your original intention in venturing into incarnate life this time can, in itself, strengthen the will to live. Self-examination is the way to this discovery. Most people understand this intuitively and admire and respect the effort as it relates to opportunity or to the lack of it.

The will to live is seldom defeated by circumstances that are difficult. It is more readily affected by the lack of self-acceptance and self-worth.

What do we gain by understanding self-worth?

You cannot learn about yourself by measuring yourself by others, basking in the praise from others, or by current moral standards. This is merely confusing. You learn about yourself by trying to understand the purpose for you of the circumstances of your life (your elements of development), all of which become yours at birth.

What do you mean by all of this?

My concern here is to convey to you a sense of what life is really all about — what is truly good and what is truly evil. This becomes a matter of quality and degree of growth, but at all levels it is the important issue. Consider the value of reciprocity.

How does reciprocity fit into this context?

In this context reciprocity means mutual respect. First

of all, you must respect another's right to be whomever he or she truly is. From this stems acceptance. You come to accept each other as you are. When this condition exists, you have reciprocity. Because true reciprocity engenders love, it inevitably involves sharing. You and I are now sharing.

Could I share with you without your willingness to share with me?
You could wish to share and act to share, but that would not be reciprocal.

Suppose I give someone a present. Haven't I shared my present whether or not I'm given something in return?
Not really. You have simply given someone a present. You would have shared it if it were received in gratitude. You see you cannot, by yourself, create a reciprocal relationship. It takes two to share something, and there must be something to share.

You have said that giving and receiving are the same things. Now you say sharing can't take place unless thanks are expressed in receiving. Please clarify.
To say "thank you" is merely the means of employing social manners to express gratitude. To give in love and to receive in love is true sharing. If the gift is not received gratefully, the purpose in giving should be examined.

There is another aspect of this subject that is helpful to understand. Reciprocity — cooperation and sharing in relationships — is not constant. It never reaches a perfect level and then stays there. On the contrary, it must be worked at minute by minute, hour by hour, day by day. It is extremely tenuous and easily destroyed. You cannot make up your mind to have such a relationship and then just have it, but you can create the possibility by doing your part. Remember, it takes two to share.

But if we try and fail, what then?

As long as you are trying, you are not failing. Even if you have failed to achieve a sharing reciprocal relationship, you will not have failed to do your part. If you question the value of making the effort, consider the opposite.

What is the opposite?

Isolation. Relationships are fundamental to life, but even though you might know this, when relationships fail the tendency is to try to control them or to retreat from them. Either of these paths leads to isolation, becoming more and more so with repetition. Total isolation, perpetual aloneness — separation from God — would surely become the final unendurable condition. Can you even imagine it?

No, I guess I can't. But you have said we are all part of the Whole. Is total isolation then possible?

Total isolation is in reality a total loss of identity—where self will becomes so complete that the individuality with which the soul was created has been lost and can no longer relate to anything outside of itself. This is the result of dedication to evil. The Self then becomes All.

Is this indeed possible?

It is theoretically, but not in actuality. The total domination of evil becomes so terrible that ultimately there is a cry for help. That cry is always answered. This is the task of discarnate servants of God.

*So the ultimate sin is really the loss of ourselves,
of the individuality with which we were created?*
Exactly. Life is a process of becoming—becoming who
you already are.

III. The Nature of Relationships

The Core

In considering relationships, just how important is the family?

The core of all relationships is the family. Everyone —single, divorced, married — is part of a family. All remarks about family therefore are to everyone. Even those who were orphaned and have no memory of their parents carry them in their physical beings, their genes, and honor their parents by honoring themselves.

Whether or not a relationship is sanctified, the birth of a child creates a family, committing the three individuals to a relationship that, acknowledged or unacknowledged, exists nevertheless. The physical family is undeniably evidenced in the genes and is the counterpart of a spiritual reality.

Could you say that all relationships are valid?

All relationships that are based on love and commitment are valid whether or not they are consummated in what is regarded as a normally sexual manner. Engendering a truly loving relationship is always constructive. Nevertheless, within the circle of the immediate family, husbands and wives, parents and children, brothers and sisters, grandparents and grandchildren, there is an obligation that transcends choice.

Why is that so?

Because you will never again be in this particular sit-

117

uation, sharing the same genes, the same circumstances, and the same set of relationships. You are dealing with past karma, good and bad, and developing new
karma. The constraints of the present situation are your
opportunity. They require of you a selfless attitude. If
you allow yourself to look at your family relationships
in this way, if you accept that they exist for a reason, you
will find yourself challenged to make them work. Even
though you may not be able to solve a problem that
exists no matter how hard you try, if you can manage
to keep a door open you will have acted in a constructive manner, with love. You will have done what you
could under the circumstances and your actions will
have raised your frequency.

In what ways can the restraints of a family situa-
tion become an opportunity?

If you accept the condition that exists as valid and therefore basically sound and justifiable, you will see that the
difficulties that present themselves are there to be solved
by you. Overcoming such constraints becomes an opportunity not only for you and your development, but also
for the development of those family members with
whom you must cope. Here you are presented with a
possibility to move forward through constructive effort,
bringing others along with you, to alleviate the difficulties with which you are faced. In this way you are creating good out of ill, a true sign of development. The
opportunity has been met.

Why is the family structure best for relationships?

The family is the most rational, cohesive, creative, and
constructive plan conceivable. Anchored in the biological nature of humans — sexual love, conception, birth,
and the nurturing of children — everything functions to

carry out physically the expression of your spiritual capacity to love. The children that result are the products of the most intimate relationship two humans can have. They are related permanently to their parents and to each other in a special way because of the shared genes.

What is your perception of childhood?

Childhood is an extension of the birthing process. It is a formative time, protected by the inborn love of parents for their children. From conception through maturation, childhood is a responsibility that parents must recognize as crucial to their own development. When there is abuse of this trust, the karmic consequences can be devastating.

Childhood is the most important time in anyone's life. The influences to which children are subjected in their formative years leave their mark throughout life. The responsibility of parents for their children cannot be overlooked without detrimental consequences that are far-reaching, affecting both children and parents on into ensuing incarnations.

What is the cause of difficult children?

Difficult children who seem impossible to handle are children, by and large, who haven't been able to feel themselves loved, who for some reason have no firm feeling of belonging, of kinship. However, the problems of the difficult child are most often karmic by nature and a cry for help from the child. Love, sympathy, and understanding are called for in all difficult circumstances. Although discipline might seem to be appropriate, one must realize that no problems are solved in this way. After all, the child has chosen you and you are to make every effort on your child's behalf. If you have a difficult child or a difficult relationship with a child, the knowledge that the child chose to come to you will almost certainly stimulate a responsive chord in you if you allow yourself to be receptive.

Why did this child come to you? What do you feel is the reason? Allowing yourself to search for the answers intuitively may very well help you to be more objective, recognizing that the child came for your help. Your best effort will be tied to your spiritual equipment — your love, your sense of truth, and your intuition.

What does it take to be a good parent?

To be a good parent is to recognize that your child, who shares your blood, has come to you for a purpose. Your role as parent is not the only role you are to play. You may also need to be teacher, companion, friend, consultant, and always intimately involved. These formative years lay a foundation for adult life, and the circumstances into which a child is born are the means of that development. The child is counting on the parents to be catalysts for the formation of a constructive incarnation.

The particular circumstances you provide as parents lived out constructively are just what your child needs for growth. How the child reacts is an indication of spiritual development. Knowing your child is the basis for your function as a parent. Achieving this understanding is your responsibility.

But can we truly know our children? Haven't you said that our spiritual needs, desires, and development are not apparent to others?

Yes, this is perfectly true. However, a loving, concerned parent can know the child's faults and the child's virtues. The parent can sense fear and its ramifications if these are present in the child, as well as general attitude, whether it is positive or negative. Since all such things are manifestations of karma, by understanding what is observed, a parent can help to change negativism into positivism, thereby assisting the child to overcome some basic problems. Love goes a long way in this effort.

Also, children themselves are not often aware of their spiritual needs either, so it is necessary to remember that you learn through your mistakes and allow them to make mistakes in order to learn more about what is right and what is wrong for them. Children who become victims of their deterrent karmic faults most often learn the hard way by suffering over and over again the consequences of their actions. It is the wise parent who realizes this and doesn't interfere. In such cases it is an act of love to step aside and allow the child to learn the hard way.

How can we understand what is most crucial about our particular family relationships?

By imaginatively linking the family to your spiritual journey through various incarnations you will sense the wisdom of the plan extended.

How?

Consider the fact that your final goal and your family members are closely linked because your family relationships, for the most part, are also relationships of goal. Those that are both become true soul mates and they remain so over and over again, incarnation after incarnation, in different guises each time but always with the same purpose — harmony and construction leading to union with God.

When do we realize that we have a need for particular parents?

The realization of your need for those you choose to be

your parents begins when you are discarnate. It is the recognition of a mutual need based on unresolved or unrealized relationships in other incarnations.

How do these fundamental relationships differ each time?

Relationships are shaped by the circumstances into which you are born. The purpose is the same, but the execution varies. Had those you chose as your parents this time lived in a different country and culture you would have faced the same basic problems and objectives, but with different circumstances in which to work them out.

Circumstances may prove to be ideal for some, but may be difficult for others depending upon preparation and development. Nevertheless, those who understand most clearly who they are and why they are where they are, those who have come best prepared, are least controlled or affected negatively by the circumstances into which they are born. They have an intuitive grasp of the value of these circumstances no matter how difficult they may seem to be.

If we are puzzled by the circumstances in which we find ourselves, how can we learn more about why we are here and to what purpose?

Ask yourself what is so important about your relationship with your parents that you needed to join them at this time. The answer to this has little to do with whether or not you happen to like them, although at some level you do most certainly love them.

Just how would I go about finding out the importance of my relationship to my parents?

By probing your inner feelings. The importance of your

relationship has to do with your reactions to your parents' efforts on your behalf. Since this time your relationship is as a child of your parents, the basis of the relationship has to do with nurturing, understanding, and love as expressed by your parents. Your need for them will be met by their love for you and the expression they give to it. Their job is to prepare you to live a constructive life, freed from your karmic problems. Through love they can give you the security to cope.

On the other hand, if your parents don't seem to understand you, don't express warmth and love toward you, you must still recognize that you have chosen them, so this situation in some way must be good for you. If you examine this thought without bias you may be able to see their problems and why they have trouble expressing themselves freely. You might find after much probing that your purpose this time is to help them. Sympathy and empathy are essential ingredients in all child – parent relationships, and they are required whether or not the parents express themselves in a loving manner. Your task as the child is to try to understand and accept your parents' limitations as well as their assets, knowing that since you chose them this particular relationship has value that must be pursued both for you and for them.

Are we to expect children to understand their parent's limitations and assets?

Many children ten years old and younger are able to size up their parents quite well, and by adolescence their parents' limitations loom more clearly than their assets! The equation usually balances out with maturity. Children are often capable of surprising mental and emotional maturity, sometimes more than their parents. Proper preparation has achieved this.

What would I do as a parent in this situation?

If you are a parent it is important to try to learn just why your children chose you. You need to examine yourself to learn what qualities in you you think were important to them when they chose you. Do you sense that you have mutual karmic problems, and if so, what are they? Do you surmise what your purpose and goal might be and those of your children as well? Have you helped them fulfill their emotional needs and desires? What clues exist in your physical beings? If you find that you love and accept them in spite of all, you have already taken a positive step toward helping them to fulfill themselves. As a parent your job is to nurture, and from that stems all that is constructive.

If, however, after much contemplation you feel you cannot cope with the problems your children represent and you wish you could choose a different situation, you must keep pursuing the problem. You must keep trying to see the situation clearly. The answer is there. If you look around, you can see many who have found it, those with circumstances that appear to be both good and bad. Remember, it is not the situation in which you find yourself that makes the difference, it is your reaction to the situation that counts. Your primary purpose as a parent is to love and accept your children as they are, and even if you never come to understand them fully, if you do this you will have been constructive in your efforts.

I don't understand. First you say we need to learn to know our children in order to help them, and then you say if we never understand them if we love and accept them we will succeed as parents?

There are degrees of success. By loving and accepting only, you are providing them with the rudiments of security. But if you can learn to know them this can help them to realize their potential supporting their efforts with both your love and understanding. A greater opportunity for development on both sides follows such effort.

Simply providing love grants your child minimal support. Getting to know your child fulfills the child – parent equation.

Destiny — Free Souls

Could you say that those who have found each other under seemingly fortuitous circumstances are destined to be together?

Those seemingly fortuitous circumstances are the working out of God's plan for them. They are truly destined to be together over and over for constructive purposes until they reach a unity of being, their hearts becoming one.

What is destiny?

Destiny is the force that impels action. It is the irrevocable Will of God functioning to bring about particular circumstances. This is recognized when people say "fulfilling your destiny," or "destined for greatness," or "destined for each other."

It is not by accident that those who are destined for each other incarnate at the same time and find each other even though they may have been born in different circumstances and places. This is true not only in love relationships, but is equally true of constructive relationships that exist to fulfill a specific purpose. One could refer to such people as "like-minded." Those who laid the foundation of democracy in the United States were such.

It sounds as though destined relationships come about quite naturally.

This is not necessarily so. Because of the circumstances

of life, destined relationships are not always easily fulfilled, winding their way through many incarnations
before culmination is reached. In a single incarnation
they may even end in tragedy. However, those involved
in such relationships are impelled to pursue their need
to be fulfilled. This need is compelling, overwhelming
everything else in importance, because those individuals can only fulfill their destinies together. Their intentions are to be fused and the result will be a joint venture
serving a constructive purpose as instruments of God.
This development has potential for everyone. It is what
all souls seek and long for, even without knowing why,
as a step toward becoming a functioning part of the
Whole.

That is why destiny is a subject for great art of all
kinds. Its hallmark is selflessness.

*The implication in destined relationships is that
two specific people seek each other out, perhaps
over many incarnations. Yet we have many relationships in even one incarnation. How could we
determine which is destined?*

Consider this: Your destiny in an incarnation is that
which God wills for you. The plan of your life and your
destiny are linked. Each plan is a stepping stone on the
path of your ultimate destiny — the fulfillment of the
needs of God in you. Each destined relationship fulfills
a requirement for your ultimate state.

All relationships are not destined relationships. A destined relationship is one that fulfills specific needs
toward spiritual growth. It may continue through many
incarnations until the needs that only this relationship
can fill are met. Each one involved in a destined relationship has something specific to give and something specific to receive — sharing essential elements of spiritual
growth.

Does everyone's destiny involve another?

In one way or another everyone's destiny involves others. It isn't always the same one, but relationships are the means of fulfilling one's destiny. Some relationships are necessarily more meaningful than others, but the destinies of all are worked out through relationships.

The ecstasies, the fulfillment, the satisfaction, the overwhelming wonder of great destined relationships, for all their overpowering impulse, are but meager examples of what we will experience when our ultimate destiny is attained — oneness with God.

Why should such destined relationships ever end in tragedy then?

Because deterrence and evil are ever ready to enter any cracks that should appear in the armor due to vulnerability to karmic problems. No matter how developed the ones involved may have become, they are not without problems until at last they have reached the ultimate state.

Could a destined relationship with another really be the potential for every person?

You think that this could not be true of everyone. In reality you are correct. However, in potential everyone could experience a destined relationship with another. This is dependent upon the quality of growth and development shared by each and the need God has for this relationship fulfilled.

So this requires a certain vulnerability to God's Will?

Yes. Those who are vulnerable to the Will of God because of their constructive efforts and accomplishments of past

lives will follow their destined paths, being open, uncon-
stricted, willing to improvise, suggestible. These qualities, this way of living, can save them from deterrent
experiences within their relationships as well as lead
them to further constructive ones.

If you are willing to follow your destiny in accordance
with God's Will for you wherever it takes you, you may
make mistakes but you will find your way.

*It seems to me that most of us are shaped by our
karma and by the society in which we find ourselves.*
That may be true of most, but there are others who are
not. They are free souls. The term "free souls" is one of
those wonderful intuitive uses of language that recog-
nizes a truth. These souls are free of the restraints that
hold most people in bondage, especially to the opinion
of others. Almost all people want to be thought well of
by someone and will do whatever is necessary to gain
such approval. Truly free souls function without this
concern because they know who they are, why they are
where they are, and what they have to do. They know
their purpose this time and they recognize that desire
for admiration is merely an expression of pride, a deterrent condition to be eschewed at any cost. Their freedom has resulted from their spiritual growth.

Can we all become free souls?
Most of you are a long way from achieving this kind of
freedom, but you can learn from those who have.

Just how do we go about trying?
First of all you are to free yourself from your compulsions
and insecurities as well as your emotional reactions to
others, by recognizing the things that enslave you — the
need to shield yourself from criticism, your need for

admiration, your dependence on others, your need to escape pressure, your fear and insecurity.

The more you can see just why you are where you are, the more you will free yourself from self-concern. The more you are freed from self-concern, the more free you will be with others.

Can we truly aspire to such an advanced role?

You have no other choice if you really want to move forward spiritually. Development toward ultimate perfection requires the utmost effort to free yourself from all of your karmic hangups. Unless you are willing to keep trying, you will find yourself caught up in deterrence, creating more and more problems to add to your karma.

Think about this carefully. To be a free soul is a true sign of spiritual development. Proper preparation is the key.

Our Bisexual Nature

You have said that our nature is bisexual. What do you mean by that?

Your *spiritual* nature is bisexual. You therefore have the capacity to alter your sex according to the requirements of an incarnation. The attributes of God the Father–Mother are present in you no matter whether you incarnate as a male or a female. The development of those attributes, however, depends upon you and upon the attendant circumstances of your various lives, including the kind of society in which you find yourself each time.

The totally female female and male male are really not the norm, but societies that project them as the ultimate female and the ultimate male to be emulated if one is to succeed within the mores of its social structure defeat the purpose of one's bisexual nature. In reality you are all mixed in your use of the two attributes of your makeup. An intuitive male and a forceful female are usually more productive just because they are functioning more fully within their dual nature. Those who blindly follow the rules for success by stressing only one facet of their sexual attributes deny themselves the realization of their true nature and thereby limit their spiritual progress or deny it altogether.

Wouldn't you say though that our society today is beginning to experience change in the traditional concept of gender roles?

There is an opening up in that direction because developed

souls are recognizing the fact that the roles of the nurturing female and the bread-winning male can be intermixed or altered for the benefit of all. Ideally this could result in both sexes developing their whole natures more fully. Without affecting their biological sexual orientation, men can feel free to function in traditional feminine as well as masculine roles, and women can feel free to function in traditional masculine as well as feminine roles.

If society could embrace this concept and organize itself around it, it would enable the family to function in a new and constructive way by allowing the father and the mother to share the responsibilities for child rearing, homemaking, and family support.

Would you say that fathers sharing in the birthing process is an example of this?

An important example. The whole process from conception to birth is an opportunity for men and women to use both their biological sexual nature and their bisexual spiritual nature simultaneously to the benefit of one another and the child who comes to them.

How can we learn to recognize our true nature?

Self-examination can go far toward revealing your true desires, your true nature, bringing you around to seeing yourself as unique, individual, and complex. This could be the beginning of spiritual growth and a new and productive life.

Does this have anything to do with relationships and, if so, how?

You have embarked on an important necessary development in relationships — the fact that you must come to experience all gradations of your sexual qualities within the context of your relationships. The attributes of maleness and femaleness are to be fully developed, refined, and perfected in each of you before you can hope to reach your ultimate goal. It is only within your relationships that you can develop and express the attributes of your spiritual bisexual nature in whatever proportion they are provided in a particular incarnation. Each incarnation, because of its goal, presents a different requirement in this regard. It is essential that you come to realize the balance within yourself each time you incarnate. Through the relationships that you have recognized as essential before returning, you are able to develop whatever capacity is needed to move you forward spiritually.

Thinking of our spiritual nature as bisexual is not an easy concept for many of us to accept.

I want you to see that we are not interested in the so-called norm. We are interested in the development of individuality. It is only in this way that one develops spiritually. To acknowledge what society accepts is all right in passing, but must not be core thinking. The spiritual aspect of your nature is a fact. That's enough. All incarnates are variations on this theme, whether they recognize it or not. In recognizing it they accept their individuality and thank God for it.

How does homosexuality fit into this picture?

Homosexuals and heterosexuals do not differ at all in this respect. Both are bisexual spiritually. Sexual orientation in the seen world depends upon the circumstances into which one is born, stemming from karmic needs and intentions.

Homosexuality is as purposeful as any other circumstance of life. However, whatever the purpose, it will be better fulfilled if the individuals understand and develop their spiritual bisexuality. Through their relationships the desires of God the Father–Mother can be enhanced.

All forms of love are acceptable to God, and a loving homosexual relationship is just that. However, promiscuous sexual behavior for gratification alone separates one from God. Responsibility in this regard varies with spiritual development.

What determines the proportion of femaleness in a male and maleness in a female?

This is a matter of frequency or spiritual development. Examples of how people tend to make use of their male and female attributes are endless, but I will give you a rule of thumb concerning this:

Maleness — Activity, strength, aggression.

Femaleness — Passivity, receptivity, intuition.

The more spiritually developed you are the more your dual nature is utilized.

Is it true that each time we enter the Place of Preparation we bring with us the trait of maleness or femaleness that was dominant in our previous incarnate life?

In the Place of Preparation the trait you bring with you each time is identified by your aura: strong color — maleness, pastel colors — femaleness.

Why would there need to be a differentiation of this kind in the Place of Preparation?

Because when you arrive your spirit reflects the outcome of your use of the attributes of whatever sex dominated your previous incarnate life.

You all are to make use of the attributes of the two

sexes over and over again in an effort to bring the spirit along on its journey toward its goal. All of these attributes in multifarious combinations contribute to spiritual growth in accordance with their use as determined by color.

You have said that even though we assume the individuality of all others while in the final state, we still retain our individual uniqueness and are always recognized for who we are. Would this uniqueness contain a special sexual orientation?

Yes, exactly. Even though by this time your bisexual nature is fully developed, your individuality dictates whether you will ultimately become intuitively active or strongly passive. The function of the particular organ of God's ultimate state of which you are to be an integral part requires certain elements to be passive and certain elements to be active, the ebb and flow that is evident throughout nature. These are fundamental conditions of life and will also be fundamental to the functioning of the perfect multifaceted evolving state of God's ultimate Being.

Then would you say that how we make use of our bisexual nature is a strong contributing factor to the success or failure of our incarnate relationships, and thus to our own spiritual development?

It is fundamental.

Are you saying that development of our bisexual nature enhances love even though that is contrary to our usual concept?

Concentration on your sexual identification as such tends to be self-limiting. The more you allow yourself to experience and express all aspects of the Love and Will of God, the more fully you will love one another. You can see for yourself that if you feel free to give and to receive, to protect and be protected, to be active and to be passive, to tolerate and be tolerated, to experience and to be experienced, your love will surely be enhanced.

Religion — Prejudice

Wouldn't it be better if there had been only one divine revelation to all people, one religion for all?
God as the All in All is impossible to comprehend, so the primary purpose of the messages brought by the great revealers is to help you to relate to a facet of God. Then, as a result of your relationship to God, you learn to relate to one another as creations of God.

During the course of many incarnations you are able to learn and experience the tenets of all of the various religions, increasing your opportunities to know and love God. Those who have profited from these opportunities relate well to those of other religions: for instance, the Christians who accept reincarnation, or the Hindus who revere Christ. Those who have not profited not only will not accept other religions as valid, but often accept only a faction of their own, or perhaps reject religion altogether.

Just because some reject religion altogether in one incarnation doesn't mean that they will reject it in another, does it?
Certainly not. It is the nature of the environment, the circumstances of development, that determines religious belief to a great extent, often detrimentally. For instance, those religions that teach children from their earliest years to believe in exclusionist concepts are apt to keep a hold on these children during that incarnation, but the circumstances of another incarnation will present entirely different obstacles and opportunities "As the

137

bough is bent" depends on spiritual development and can only apply to one incarnation at a time.

But what about those who are searching, those who respond to your teaching for instance? When we say "Crucial Concepts" are we not in danger of creating another orthodoxy?

These are concepts — an invitation to conceive. We wish only to reinforce the fundamental truths of the great religions by showing you not only their reasonableness, but their reasonableness together as one concept. Life must make sense to people, the effort to live a good life must seem purposeful as indeed it is. The way we are suggesting that you do this is through your own self — your love, your sense of truth, and your intuition. Those who have recognized both the value and the limitations of various organized religions during past incarnations are able to embrace both the opportunity for good and the responsibility for evil inherent in any belief.

Even though one can be appealed to through both the emotions and the mind, it is the heart where God dwells that determines true spiritual growth and, therefore, what you are meant to believe.

Our effort is to put forth truth that will be understandable and acceptable to those who are ready and willing to obey God's Will, recognizing and following the spirit behind moral law, knowing it to be superior to the letter of the law.

If all revelations are of God, it makes it difficult to understand "no man cometh unto the Father but by Me." [1]

This is true in a cosmic sense since all the great revela-

---

[1] John 14.6

tions come from the same source. However, it also becomes understandable to all through reincarnation. Many incarnates don't have the opportunity to follow Christ's teaching because they are born into a Judaic environment, a Hindu environment, an Islamic environment, etc., learning God's truth from different points of view. Through reincarnation, however, all eventually are born into a Christian environment and in different incarnations come to experience various aspects of Christianity in the same way they have experienced various aspects of all other religions.

Accepting one religion in an incarnation helps acceptance of another religion in another incarnation, receiving different insight in each. The heart can always respond to truth.

How do you explain the evil done in the name of religion?

As well as bringing out the best in people, religion often seems to bring out the worst. Since those who are deterrent and evil cannot defeat God, they try to usurp His Kingdom on earth by appropriating the Word. When they identify with a religion, any apparent threat to that religion in their minds is a threat to them. Therefore, any kind of punishment employed in eliminating that threat is justified in their minds because they think that it is the religion that is being defended. People have been maimed and murdered in the name of religion; wars have been fought over religion. However, the death of martyrs (great souls infused with God's Love and God's Grace) often generates enough Constructive Force to renew the Word debased by hatred and malice.

Isn't it the differences in religions that causes this?

It is not the differences in religions that causes the problems, but pride and its aspects — fear, hatred, malice,

negativism in all of its elements — the very problems
that religion is intended to overcome.

You must eventually come to see that none of the great
religions is to be considered wrong, since all of them contain aspects of God's basic truth.

Then what is it that is wrong?

What is wrong is the attempt to own a religion, to possess it, to define and confine it, to follow the letter of
moral law instead of its spirit. This is the antithesis of
oneness — the basis of our relationship to God and to one
another. Religion in its purity is to serve as a means to
that end.

Would you say that prejudice is learned here or do we come with it?

Prejudice is obviously learned, but unless it falls on fer-
tile karmic ground (past unresolved pride), it will not
become deep rooted and will usually disappear as one
becomes adult and experiences the vicissitudes of life.
However, prejudice that is karmic (learned and prac-
ticed in past incarnations) often achieves powerful
dynamics, drawing in those whose prejudice has been
learned in their present incarnation. We speak especially
of those who are too weak to resist and those who have
a need to bolster their own egos by downgrading and
denouncing others. The object against which people are
prejudiced is always secondary to their need to prejudge.

How does mass prejudice develop?

The appalling phenomenon of mass prejudice spreads,
with the help of Deterrent Force, from those whose prejudice is karmic (those who have brought the deterrence
with them) to those who are learning it now. If there is

no vulnerable group for their hatred they will create one
espousing prejudice through pride.

What is the cause of prejudice?

During a person's history of reincarnating, many differing kinds of life are experienced, both sexes, heterosex-
uality, homosexuality, various colors, races, and
nationalities. To know that after you reincarnate your
color and your sex are part of the circumstances of life
is to know that all such varying experiences are intended
for your good. If you, in your present incarnation, are
prejudiced against different races or have difficulty
accepting another way of life, it probably comes from an
unresolved experience in a previous life to which you are
reacting. On the other hand, if you are at ease with conditions other than your own, you have certainly profited
from your previous experiences. Any and all established
prejudices must be experienced as the object of prejudice and the lesson learned in future incarnations.

Just who is the prejudiced person?

The prejudiced person may have been either the perpetrator or the recipient of prejudice as a result of which
unresolved problems remain. Or such a person may fear
and be ill prepared for new experiences — the karmic
legacy of a closed mind. All such people should try to
imagine themselves as others, concentrating on the
present, to try to see things as they really are.

On the other hand, if you find yourself with an unreasoning prejudice, it could come from previous devastating experiences that were unresolved. In this case it
may be well to allow yourself to experience imaginatively your anger and hatred and allow it to take its own
shape. Imagine yourself as both the perpetrator and the

recipient. Either way the root of prejudice is almost always fear stemming from pride from which anger and hatred are generated. If you allow yourself to experience the fear, that act of courage may well overcome your unreasoning feelings and help to resolve at least some of your prejudices.

Are you talking about imagination or past-life regression as practiced in certain therapy?

It isn't possible to draw a distinction since imagination is a reality that can lead to past-life regression. However, although complete regression in the right hands can be valuable in grasping the source of long-standing phobias such as prejudice, it should not be regarded as necessary to accomplish this. You are already well equipped with your imagination, intuition, and sense of truth to deal with this problem.

Since it is evidently valuable to experience different races, colors, etc., is it then unwise to intermarry with another race or religion and thereby blur distinctions?

Intermarriage with mutual respect and love is desirable. It is an act of courage that obviates prejudice.

The courage to face it out can ultimately lead to acceptance. The more people are willing to follow their hearts no matter where it leads them, the better for all concerned. Familial love can break down prejudice and allow people to see more clearly , understanding the importance of accepting things as they are.

How should the differences be handled?

Disparate traditions are to be respected and observed. Children are to be helped to understand the similarities and the differences in varying cultures. From this they learn that it is fear coming from ignorance about others that causes prejudice.

I wonder why differences cause such problems?

It isn't the differences themselves, since if there were no differences people would tend to create them. The problem is the way people regard differences of any kind —whether they reach out in love or retreat into fear and hate. You should value your differences beginning with your individuality, and you should also value what you have in common starting with life and the planet earth.

From your vantage point, what are the important things we have in common?

You are all human beings, children of God. You all possess the same spiritual equipment — your love, your sense of truth, and your intuition. You are each individual and you are all related. Just how you use these common elements depends upon your perceptions, stemming from growth and development. Some, due to karmic problems, refuse to extend love, to see truth, or to utilize their intuition. When this happens, deterrence and negativism control relationships. Time is often a healer in instances of prejudice. You learn by your mistakes.

What about self-prejudice?

Since your karmic difficulties are with you when you are born, it is easy to mistake them for your real selves and so fall into a pattern of self-deprecation and self-hatred. In both cases you are prejudging. You are forming an opinion on the basis of insufficient evidence. You don't see the whole picture, seeing only what is wrong, not including what is right.

What is the outcome of such prejudgment?

Unfortunately, prejudging yourself in this way becomes a self-fulfilling prophecy. You are likely to become what you assume you are. Nevertheless, consider the fact that no one reincarnates for negative reasons. The reasons for which you decided to reincarnate were positive. Your intentions were right as you saw them. You must have decided to overcome some of your karmic load, build a stronger character, improve and mend some of your relationships, and work to achieve your purpose in coming.

If you try you can rediscover that self whom you've known before, your real self, and that real self will prove all that is being said here. It is easier to criticize the self you have let yourself become — the self of self-will — than to recreate your real self. With a grievous karma this becomes difficult to achieve, but with God's help it is possible.

How could this be done?

Try to imagine why you came. Imagine this in the context of your relationships and circumstances of your life, your elements of development. Trust your true heart feelings where God dwells and your spiritual equipment, the essence of your spiritual being, to show you why you are who you are and where you are. If and when you accomplish this, you will gradually begin to relate to a self you may not have known existed, a self who can do the difficult things you think you can't do.

Your relationship to yourself and to God are paralleled. You cannot become constructive without God.

Sphere of Influence

What is the difference between within our sphere of influence and throughout it?

As you sit and receive this now, you are functioning throughout your sphere of influence. The vitality you bring to the work defines the extent of the function. Although we have tended to say within our sphere of influence, if you consider this more closely you see that *within* implies boundaries that do not always exist.

Just how does functioning throughout our sphere of influence play itself out?

The energy you put to your thoughts and deeds is felt by others in accordance with the amount and concentration of that energy. If your thoughts and deeds are moderate, their effect will be moderate. If the distilled essence of your thoughts is powerful, their effect will be far more extensive. Your sphere of influence then is determined by the concentrated power that goes into your thoughts and deeds.

How does our sphere of influence function?

The method of functioning is through relationships. That is implicit in the phrase "sphere of influence." Although it has its limitations as an analogy, the thought of a stone dropped in a pond, causing a widening circle of ripples to become concentric with the circles from other stones, does seem to serve to illustrate the way in which the sphere of influence functions. The heavier the

145

stone (power of thought) from which the ripples emanate, the larger the sphere of influence, whether for good or for ill. It is important, however, not to confuse the size of the sphere of influence with merely knowing many people. You may know many people and be unaffected by them, and they by you. Sphere of influence has to do with the profound effect for good or for ill that you have on others, starting with your family and moving outward.

First you say that our sphere of influence, the extent of the effect of our efforts on others, is determined by the power of our thoughts and deeds. Now you say there are many who are not affected by our efforts at all. How do you justify those statements?
You should see that all of your efforts couldn't affect everybody. Those who are affected by them are those who are on the same wavelength, those who are related by blood or goal. Those who are not affected have not had a meaningful relationship with you.

Then our influence is limited after all?
No. I'm saying that all those with whom you have had an affinity, incarnate or discarnate, are directly affected by what you think and do.

Why is it important to consider our sphere of influence at all?
It is well to examine your relationships in the light of your sphere of influence because it is this for which you will be answerable. You will be accountable for yourself and your own sphere of influence. Remember, this doesn't stop with your direct effect on others but continues on through all those who are subsequently affected.

You, on the other hand, function also in the sphere of others, and they bear a responsibility toward you.

Please explain how this works.

Influence is a magnetic field that attracts varying degrees of frequency. The vibrations that an individual emits attract other vibrations. Therefore, we are concerned not merely with the extent of the vibrations, but with the kind of vibrations. Are they regular or irregular? Are they a force for good or for ill?

I'm still unclear about just what our sphere of influence is.

I would like you to consider this: Your sphere of influence is really the present you. Your persona, this specific incarnate personality that you are playing out now, is in reality as palpable as anything you can see and hear. It has an emotionalism, varying with its own power, that is either constructive or deterrent. If it is dynamic, it may well linger on earth after your incarnation is over. This is not merely memory. It is animate to the extent that strong vibrations continue to emanate from it. Others, in other times and places, may be affected by it just as you have been affected by distant lives. Consider for instance the Twenty-Third Psalm. When it is recited one is immediately in a sphere of influence that has extended over thousands of years.

Here you say that our sphere of influence is really our persona, our personality that influences and even lingers on. But as you have also said, our persona, personality and persona differ with each incarnation and it is our individuality that is enduring. Help me understand this.

Think of your individuality as permanent, and your persona and personality changing with each incarnation, but contributing to your effectiveness and influence nevertheless. Then you will see that the persona and personality extend the effects of one's individuality, coloring it in one way or another. Your persona and personality are the outward means through which your inner being is expressed, differing with each incarnation. They are the means through which your individuality functions, creating your sphere of influence.

Surely our personality is influenced by our genes and circumstances of life.

That's true. However, the genes and circumstances of the life of a Hitler could have resulted in an ordinary Austrian businessman. It was the karmic inner being propelled by Deterrent Force that brought about the evil that emanated through an ever-enlarging sphere of influence. The influence no longer has dynamics, but the memory lingers on and serves to teach us.

Can the influence of a person also be felt in the other world?

Remember, this is all one world. The sphere of influence is not limited by time or space. Yours extends here, and ours extends there. You are influenced by us as we are by you. The key is vulnerability — sensitivity to influence. The more sensitive you are to our influence, the more you live in our world and we live in yours. Think about this.

What do you mean by vulnerability?

When you are able to acknowledge our existence, when you think of us in the present, when you pray to us and for us as we do for you, when you include us in your thoughts, you are vulnerable to the reality of the two worlds as one profiting from your understanding of truth.

Should we think of ourselves as being in your sphere of influence?

You will benefit from it if you do. The realization that you are still in the sphere of influence of your loved ones who have gone on will help you to live the life you are destined to live.

How?

Through imagination and heightened consciousness, through faith, through dreams and the pattern of your life, through opening up to receive help — through love.

IV. Relationships Today

Behavioral Changes

What is it that makes love, sex, and choice compatible with God's Will for us?

Commitment. Any relationship that is truly loving is constructive. However, uncommitted relationships, while seeming to liberate, tend to isolate. Uncommitted and loving are contradictory terms. You cannot truly love your wife, your work, your country, or your God without in some way committing yourself.

Are you really saying that we can't love someone or something without being committed?

I am saying that true love goes hand in hand with the desire to commit yourself to that person or that thing. If you are unable to give yourself in trust to a person or a cause, your love for that person or that cause is not true. It is a fickle aberration of the God-given emotion.

But whether you like it or not, in some ways you are already committed. Biologically, men, women, and their children function as one. Even if you don't choose to have a family, you are still part of a family. Just as the biological function can't be separated from the emotional, so the emotional can't be separated from the spiritual.

How do men, women, and their children function as one?

They are related by blood and most often by goal. Because of this they are a unit. The children have chosen their parents for their own spiritual growth, and the

153

interaction between children and parents creates a unity
of purpose — a oneness of function.

How would you define the family?

The family is God's basic design for human relationships. It insures that as souls reincarnate, they will be
related to others, they will be born into relationships.
The survival of the family is not a moral issue; it is a
necessity for the emotional and spiritual growth of those
returning to the incarnate world.

When it comes to relationships, I think most people need help in a practical way.

That is exactly what we want to offer, but the practical
way is not personal advice. It is much more practical
than that. It is universal advice to which everyone can
relate, rendering it inescapably personal. Remember,
just as it is true that you need a clear conscience to grow,
it is also true that a clear conscience differs with each
person. So it is with relationships.

The elements that make good relationships — your
individual character, circumstances, and karma — differ
with each one of you. In committing to another you are
committing not just to the incarnate persona, but to the
eternal being. Therefore, the most helpful thing that you
can do is to try to understand who your loved ones really
are and why they are with you.

To understand is the important issue here: not to
figure out or decode, but truly to understand — to believe
in and encourage their intention in coming, to help overcome difficult karma and rejoice in beneficial karma. If
your own commitment is first of all to God's Love and
God's Will, you will learn to understand your loved ones
as well as yourself, including your own hope in reincarnating this time and your own karmic struggles and
development.

How does the prevalent extended family — "your children, my children, and our children," divorced people with children marrying — fit into the scheme of things?

Here we have a complex pattern of relationships: those who are related by blood and goal intermingled with those who are not truly related at all. Some may be related to one parent and some to the other, and some to both. And those who are related to one parent may very well be involved with another family of their other parent.

This situation is rife with problems of all kinds. Nevertheless it must be seen as part of the circumstances of life and therefore potentially beneficial. To recognize the construction that lies beneath all circumstances is to benefit from life, bringing spiritual development.

Should our primary commitment be to our children?

Your primary commitment should be to God's Will for you. Allow God to function through you and no matter how difficult the circumstances seem to be, you will be enabled to find constructive solutions to them. Other commitments may be broken, be allowed to dissolve, or may never have been real commitments at all. Whatever the cause, the concentration should always be on construction.

What happens if one person tries to do that and the other is bent on deterrence?

You must remember that God's commitment to you is unfailing. In times of great stress, remember also that your efforts are paralleled in the unseen world. You are never alone in your efforts toward constructive commitment.

Is sexual practice influenced by our circumstances of development?

It certainly is. But we are concerned more precisely that you understand that the degree and kind of sexuality with which you are born is a purposeful part of your development. What is right for you is not necessarily right for someone else. This is not accidental. It is what you need for your own development, so it should help you to understand yourself and be tolerant, accepting, and not envious or critical of others. You can neither make rules or be guided by them, but must find the answer for yourself through the use of love, your sense of truth, and your intuition.

How can adolescents, confronted with the demands of their sexual natures, find answers for themselves?

This will probably be a matter of trial and error even when there has been good preparation for an incarnation and fortunate relationships and circumstances.

Furthermore, even though your society has removed most of the traditional safeguards, adolescents have special qualities to equip them for the changes they are undergoing. They are naturally idealistic, romantic, and adventuresome — God-given qualities with which to start out on the search for love and an independent life. It is the corruption of the natural idealism of youth that defeats some young people before they even begin their search.

What has birth control contributed to the sexual revolution?

Separating sex from procreation gives the opportunity of choice. But because it is artificial (outside of nature), it therefore must evolve its own ethics. This can be done individual by individual, acting with the guidance of your spiritual equipment.

Birth control expands freedom, but in so doing increases responsibility. If these two aspects go hand in hand, the effect is positive; if not, it is of course negative. The most positive and necessary freedom that has resulted is the trend toward emancipation of women.

How does this affect relationships?

The ideal relationship was once the protector and the protected, thus ensuring family growth and stability. Now a new ideal relationship must be built around the concept of sharing rather than dependency — sharing the obligations and the opportunities of both the workplace and the home.

Please amplify this thought.

If you will consider the fact that birth control limits the outcome of sexual practice, you will see that present conditions in the Western world particularly are altered because of it. By holding yourself responsible to function in accordance with God's Will, utilizing love, your sense of truth, and intuition to guide you, you will be able to put into practice your concept of what is right for you. This will result in an ethic acceptable to you and to God. You are not acting blindly. You are utilizing your spiritual equipment to arrive at the solution for you.

That sounds as though everything is under control, there is no problem.

Under ideal conditions you are right. However, the compelling nature of sex can quickly override a person's true feelings. In this way sex is often separated from love, which, along with procreation, is its reason for being. When this happens one loses touch with one's true self — the soul. Were this tendency carried to the extreme it would be possible to produce a soulless society — a hell on earth. However, this is not likely to happen because sex, love, and the ability to choose when to have children, or indeed even *if* to have children, need not be mutually incompatible.

Is it possible that the biochemical revolution that is taking place today will affect behavior in our relationships?

There is no doubt that the biochemical revolution has altered life fundamentally. As your knowledge of the physical universe increases, so has your power to change it. As we discussed in *The Challenge of Evil*, you can be facing another Dark Age or an Age of Enlightenment. That is up to you and your behavior. You must, therefore, concern yourselves not with the inevitability of change, but with its consequences. In many ways, including human relationships, these changes are already developing.

How has birth control altered our behavior?

The problem here is not that birth control separates the act from its intended outcome, but that it often separates it from its true motivation — love. This, of course, is not new, but its acceptance as the norm blurs society's vision of the ideal. As a result, instead of having strong, stable, and lasting relationships, the tendency is toward numerous failed relationships resulting in a society of isolated individuals.

The meaningless, careless sexual encounters made possible by birth control are also resulting in increasing numbers of single-parent children. Instead of birth control being used with precaution to liberate women, it is creating a new kind of situation, especially among the very young — that of a single mother.

We are seeing some unimaginable changes such as

surrogate mothers and sperm banks. What about these?

These are moral problems. All moral problems must be decided by the individual guided by conscience and spiritual equipment. In a free society there is always the danger of misuse for personal gain.

Are you saying that parenting, even as remote as artificial insemination from a sperm bank, must some day be realized and resolved?

Since parenting and the relationships made possible because of it are the fundamental plan for life on earth, can you imagine that parenting could be ignored or would have no consequences? This is mankind's most sacred trust.

But not everyone is a parent.

No one is a parent in every incarnation. There are other paths to follow and other karmic legacies to work out. But all are parents at one time or another.

It seems as though we're being caught up in behavior, the consequences of which we don't understand. What is the hope?

Out of need resulting from the anguish caused by confused moral values, a surge of energy is beginning to break through from the unseen world, reaching those in the seen world who are willing to accept the reality of reincarnation as an element of both Christianity and Judaism. It is not the purpose of this divulgence to make this historically reasonable. That has already been done.[1]

---

[1] See *Reincarnation: A New Horizon in Science, Religion and Society* by Sylvia Cranston and Carey Williams (Crown Publishers, New York, 1984).

The power of these beliefs can transform the way people use the knowledge resulting from scientific advances.

This is our hope: Through reading and talking about it, trying to make it both real and reasonable to people in their everyday lives, a change will be brought about.

To accomplish this there must be two things — motivation, and acceptance of individual responsibility. This can come from an understanding and acceptance of reincarnation. This achievement is our purpose.

When you refer to yourself you tend to use we instead of I. Why is this?

I think it is well for you to bear in mind that there are many individuals here helping in this effort. Individual effort, both in the seen and the unseen world united in one purpose, is the key to the future. The teaching of reincarnation channeled from spiritual forces to individuals who are willing to try to understand their lives as part of a continuing process has virtually unlimited power to change the world.

What would be the actual outcome of such effort?

This willingness, if pursued, could be a positive change capable of counteracting all of the negative changes taken together, even dominating and overcoming evil. The function of the Law of Parallels, plus efforts from those of us in the unseen world, will aid you who are willing to understand changing developments as opportunities and challenges. God did not create the world to be destroyed. He created it to be an ever-renewing home to which His children can return and help one another to progress toward oneness with Him.

Family

Isn't the concept of the family as the basis for the development of relationships hindered by the proliferation of unstructured relationships?

You are right. However, we must expand on the family concept because in spite of all, it is the most important element in spiritual growth. Even though you may not feel kindly toward members of your family, they are kin and you must recognize that kindness and kin stem from the same source. The words themselves tell the story. The concept that kindness and kinship are one and the same stems from an ancient understanding of the nature of relationships. The thought and the word stem from the same root. Indeed, it is in our nature to treat our kin with kindness, an aspect of love. If you don't you are not allowing your higher self (the God in you) to function. You are allowing your lower (temporal) self to assume authority over you.

In ancient times people acted kindly only toward their kin. Toward all others they were confrontational. Now, however, the proliferation of self-will has brought about a lack of responsibility toward and attachment to the family. The sense of importance of the family has been lessened due to the imposition of self-concern, causing a lack of understanding of the long family attachments that have existed over many, many incarnations toward the same people, and the importance of these attachments to the ultimate goal in life. There is much to be gained by loving, or at least relating to, your kin, as well

161

as being responsible to and for them not only because of the long-standing relationships that they represent, but also because of the ultimate outcome of your purpose.

How would you define relationships between parents and children today?

To a large degree the situation is one of alienation. Every society has its flaws regarding the care of children. In some societies they are over-protected, in others they are under-protected, but new and entirely different problems are present today. Children's lives are becoming detached from their parents' lives, whether they are in a structured situation away from home, or a totally unstructured and sometimes unsupervised situation at home where an impersonal medium — the television —takes a dominant role in shaping their discernment and aspirations.

Is this a problem of the sexual revolution?

Although this would seem to be so, that isn't really the case. In fact it could be beneficial to children if parents were to share equally in caring for them as well as supporting them. To gain time for this, however, the whole family would often have to sacrifice materially, which leads to the real problem — materialism.

You say that materialism is the problem, but when both parents feel they must work in order to support a family, what can they do?

They are to consider the emotional security of their children above all else. They must understand the truth about the need their children have for them as parents and that their children have chosen them, so they owe them their best effort at parenthood. Those parents who think that money will solve all of their family problems are wrong. Love and understanding are far more necessary to a child than money. Once parents get involved with the money syndrome, there is never enough. Money then becomes the end rather than a means to the end.

I am not saying that people should stay at the poverty level in order to spend more time with their children. I suggest that if they put the welfare of their children first on their list of priorities, if they give them love and understanding, if they seek harmony in their relationship with them, knowing that their children need their particular qualities for their own development, what is required monetarily will come to them. By being responsible for their children in this way, they will have set their priorities in accordance with God's Will for them, so out of the circumstances that develop the necessary wherewithal will materialize. What they need they will get.

Are you saying that the needed money will just appear if we do right by our children?

I am saying that your capabilities and talents will become more fully realized in financial terms if you live according to God's Will for you as a parent. The harmony that surrounds such effort will bring constructive results that will benefit all concerned, particularly the security of your children.

Isn't it important to give our children as many of the advantages science has provided us as we can?

You must try to sort this out. If the acquisition of all that the scientific revolution makes possible is more important than family relationships, the family will become the victim of the society it has created. The pressures are so powerful that they will fill the vacuum caused by absent parents, leaving the children floundering.

Is it possible that others trained in child care could do the job better than many parents?

To some extent, but this is not a question of efficiency but of blood relationship. In spite of the difficulties entailed in the decision, the primary reason we reincarnate is to develop and possibly rectify certain relationships. We have chosen our parents, we have accepted the circumstances of our lives.

Just how important is this?

To get some conception of its importance, think of the courage it takes to be born and and start out as a helpless infant. This act of courage usually remains intact and comes to be understood through childhood, in fact throughout life, as the will to live.

Is it important to the spirit to relate to both parents?

Although you choose both of your parents, it is often the case that one is your reason for reincarnating — a close relationship in other incarnations that you now need to develop and make grow or perhaps make amends for. This is part of the whole purposefulness of life. However, even though you may be drawn emotionally to only one parent, it is important to recognize the biological significance of both. Otherwise a vacuum is created where there should be a parent. Your heritage — mental, emotional, and physical — is important for self-development. To be able to relate in love to the source of the qualities you derived from both of your parents is helpful in learning about yourself.

It doesn't always happen though, even in the natural course of events. What about orphans?

This is a separate question usually involving karma.

However, children should not be deprived of whatever knowledge is available concerning the biological parents. This could help them to understand themselves and also help adoptive parents to understand their true role. Children in foster homes have a more difficult time relating because of the lack of commitment involved in such a situation. Whether or not there is a physical relationship between child and parents, the parents are part of the child's consciousness, and even though the child may not even know the parents' identity, the parents are nevertheless living in the child — appearance, capabilities, temperament, etc. Even though much may be lost if one hasn't known one's parents, that fact doesn't sever the relationship. It just postpones it. This will be realized in the Place of Preparation and resolved in future incarnations. If the separation was caused by death, the reunion will be joyful. If the separation was deliberate, it will be more difficult.

Is the will to live something we've had to develop each time in the Place of Preparation prior to reincarnating, or is it something we've had since our creation, a part of our essential being?

The courage it takes to reincarnate each time stems from an inner feeling, an urge to grow and develop in accordance with God's Will in spite of the difficulties it may present. The desire to move forward is recognized as essential to our being, and when reincarnating becomes the obvious next step, one takes the plunge with a combination of anticipation and trepidation. The will to live is an essential part of our being, but it can be strengthened by purpose. As an incarnation is seen as truly important and necessary for growth, the will to live all problems through will be strengthened.

The infant seems to be at a tremendous disadvantage. Is this compensated for in any way?

Parental love. It is part of our nature — it is inborn. It is needed to insure that the souls reentering incarnate life as infants receive the nurturing they require. Normally an infant comes bringing love and trust and the parents respond with love and trust. This is usually true in spite of karmic problems.

What is the unique benefit of parental nurturing?

The nurturing process is for the benefit of both parents and children, and should bond them together in love. That is God's plan, and if all parents lived in accordance with it it would become a reality. Even though both parents and children come with many karmic problems, the bond between them, forged during the nurturing process, usually withstands the stress. Parental love is a hardy plant, difficult to destroy, although some parents do succeed in doing so.

Isn't it true that there are some homes so fraught with deterrence that it seems as though the children would be better off elsewhere?

It is true that just as the potential for benefit is greater in a family than anywhere else, so is the potential for harm. Because of this it sometimes becomes imperative to find another place for the children to live. This can work out constructively, but it cannot be regarded as a final solution since it is only delaying the resolution of the relationship until another time.

If strangers are nurturing the children, what does this do to the concept of the family?

In this respect it is well to remember that you who are

incarnate are all one family. The children are yours —
your responsibility. They must all be cared for. As you
see a child in need, it is your responsibility to do what
you can to alleviate the problem. As society redefines
itself and reincarnation is better understood, the family
will take on new meaning. When we speak of God the
Father–Mother, we are recognizing that there are two
wholly individual aspects of God that function as one.
So it is with the family. We are not only our brother's
keeper, but also our brother's children's keeper.

Are there other aspects of the family to consider?

A nation is also a family — a family encompassing qualities of traits and purpose. Among the oriental nations,
for instance, the traits of the Chinese and Japanese are
recognizably different, just as among the occidental
nations one can denote the differences between the English and the French without hesitation. The purpose of
the United States, for instance, is personal freedom, and
so it must freely choose to care for its children. All
nations are to do this, each in its own way. Failure to do
this results in loss of freedom of choice and negativism.

Is there a guiding principle for parental behavior?

The guiding principle for parents is to understand and
use their spiritual equipment. If they are guided by their
love, sense of truth, and intuition, their influence on
their children will be constructive, avoiding the deterrence of emotionalism. Rather than trying to run their
children's lives, they will instead teach them to be guided
by their own spiritual equipment. This gives breathing
space, allowing for individuality to express itself within
family life.

It seems to me that belief in continuing relation-

ships requires a greater leap of the imagination than most can muster. What do you say?

I say that the concept is not as foreign to you as you might think. Examining your inner feelings can give rise to this understanding. You have known this truth for all of your discarnate life, which spans a far greater length of time than that of your incarnate lives. The discarnate memory retains this truth. Those who learn to live in accordance with their inner feelings are able to agree.

How could the sexual revolution free men and women to live the roles most beneficial for them and their children?

The possibilities of the sexual revolution are for an ideal society in which men, women, and children are equally respected and loved. Sexual energy, understood for what it is — God's gift to those who do not separate it from its spiritual essence, love — will be both respected and full-hearted. Openness and lack of inhibition will result, and these will free people to be themselves in their relationships.

The function of birth control will prove beneficial, limiting the global population to the capacity of the earth to sustain it as well as allowing the size of the family to be responsive to the capability and desires of the parents.

Women will be freed to use all of their abilities fully, including the ability to have children under circumstances that society creates in recognition of the true meaning and value of the birthing process.

Men will be free to function more fully in the nurturing of new life. They will also be able to develop abilities other than those needed to make a living.

What about the family?

It is possible that the basic wisdom of the family will be

understood as God's design for human relationships, encompassing both worlds. Then both difficulties and blessings in human relationships will be recognized as challenges to be met. The family will not only survive but flourish, not because it is respectable or right, but because it is the most vital and important way to grow through relationships. It harbors relationships through blood lines.

The truth in intuitive feelings will be acknowledged and will be trusted as guides to marriage partners, eliminating many of the mistakes made because of marriage for the wrong reasons. The belief that children have chosen their parents will help both parents and children to understand each other and their relationship. It is possible that enough developed men and women will be sufficiently sobered by what is resulting from the sexual revolution, particularly in the field of genetic engineering, that they will assume responsibility for bringing in the new age.

Is there more to consider about possibilities?

I would like you to consider this: think of relationships as in a state of flux and you will see that the possibilities are endless for both good and ill. The situation with women today has been a necessary move toward a balance with that of men. Equality of the sexes is needed to bring about better conditions for all. Equality in this sense has to do with the spiritual aspects of human development, with each sex continuing to adhere to its function in the scheme of reincarnation. The development until now is merely a glimpse of what could be. Although present relationships are not necessarily good, this is a passing phase in the development of the human spirit through relationships. Humility in the sight of God is a necessity for all, both sexes alike. But true humility cannot be reached until each one is able to realize the

potential individuality and uniqueness granted at creation. In potential, men and women are equal in the sight
of God. This equality must be acknowledged in the sight
of mankind.

Men are to come to see that women are not only a biological necessity, but a spiritual necessity as well. The
interaction of male–female qualities is essential to the
working out of spiritual development. God is our
Father–Mother, and we all have experienced both maleness and femaleness on earth. Wholeness is achieved
through the blending of male and female qualities in
each one. Respect for the opposite sex is essential to spiritual development.

**The present quandary in human relationships
doesn't seem to grant this possibility.**
Out of this quandary much that is good can come about.
As an antidote to aggression there will be those who see
the value in mutual respect, each for the other. Slowly
but surely both men and women will learn to value each
other as well as see the need for each other. Out of this,
love will gradually surface and dominate relationships.
People will come to love and respect themselves, and out
of that will come love and respect for others.

**There must be more to the possibilities in relation-
ships than mutual love, respect, and harmony.**
You are correct. All of mankind needs to grasp its fundamental function to grow toward spiritual perfection.
To do this it is necessary to recognize your faults and set
about to correct them. These imperfections are karmic
and must be mended through your relationships. The
problems that develop in relationships separate those
involved from the love of God.

The subject is possibilities in relationships. The possibilities are beyond measure because the ultimate goal in relationships is oneness with God. In order to be able to reach this goal, you need to grasp the concept of harmony in function. Our ultimate state will require us to function in complete harmony with all others in order to achieve wholeness with the mystical body of which we are to be a minute integral element.

What must we know about harmony in function?
To achieve harmony in function you must be aware not only of your incarnate relationships, seeking constructive solutions to your problems with them, but also of your discarnate relationships, for whom you must pray for their continuing development.

What responsibility do we have from day to day for our discarnate relationships?
You need to remind yourself that those discarnates whom you love — parents, grandparents, siblings, loved ones, friends — exist and are ready to cooperate with your efforts whenever called upon. It is not only the Law of Parallels that responds in kind to your constructive efforts, but your discarnate relationships are able to help you, too, whenever they are needed.

What form does this help take?
From their efforts for you it is possible to receive the necessary energy and ability to concentrate in order to see things clearly.

Just what should we do to get this response?
You should ask for help from those you love. The help will then be channeled to the matter at hand. If you include your discarnate loved ones in your thoughts, concerning yourself with their progress and development, you are

opening the channel through which they can respond
to your needs. In this way their reality becomes a part
of your reality — a benefit to both of you.

What about harmony with my incarnate loved ones?

This is a moment-to-moment need on your part. Seek
harmony in all incarnate situations and you will be functioning according to God's Will for you.

The discarnate relationships you refer to, do you mean only those in the Place of Preparation?

Constructive communication is possible only between
the Place of Preparation and earth.

What about those who may be in the Place of Self-Deception or the Lower Regions?

They could influence you only if you indulge in karmic
weaknesses, leaving you vulnerable.

But I don't know where my discarnate loved ones are.

This is true. But as percentages go, they are not likely
to have ended up deterrent or evil. If you pray for them,
they will benefit no matter where they are. Through your
prayers, you can help them even in spite of themselves.
They may not be able to help you, but you will be able
to help them.

Do you really see all of this as a likely possibility?

I see it as an inevitable possibility, but not for some time
to come. The present trend toward dispersed, isolated,
and meaningless relationships will continue for a long

time. But at the same time, gradually a new vision will emerge. Enlightened, loving men and women, with the courage and imagination to understand the opportunity life presents, will know what it really means to relate to one another and to their children.

Day-by-Day Relationships

Even though we are all part of a family, many of us grow up to pursue other ways of life. Will you deal with this?

Not separately, because it is not the kind of relationship that is important, but the quality of the relationship. The family with children is universal. Every other kind of relationship is individual, resulting from personal karma and/or choice.

How are we to judge these relationships?

If you know in your heart that a relationship — whatever it may be — is right for you, that it is constructive for you and your partner, then it is right. There are no rules except your heart feelings. What is right for one can be wrong for another. However, it is well to understand the nature of sexuality. The sexual act can bond, even though momentarily, spirits as well as bodies. All sexual encounters affect to some extent the spirit's sense of its own individuality. Perfect individuality is our ultimate goal, and true love relationships help to define and refine that sense of individuality. Casual sexual relationships blur it, and deterrent sexual relationships — neurotic or compulsive, long-term or short-term — do serious damage to the soul's ability to know itself and grow in a particular incarnation.

What do you say about our day-by-day relationships?

Day-by-day relationships carry with them the idea of

174

now. The quality of life you achieve day by day determines how you recreate and define yourself. Your sexual nature, even though it may be expressed overtly, is a manifestation of God's creativity. It is a God-function — God present in you.

If you remember this and allow God to be expressed through you, the result will be constructive. This vital force may express itself through your love for another, for humanity, for art, for nature.

What is the significance of "now" in relationships?

Your relationship now (of the moment) is your only active relationship — it is your opportunity. Right now stop whatever else you are doing and consider this. Realize the importance of living constructively now, aware of the immortal nature, however infinitesimal it may seem to you, of your day-by-day relationships.

Since we have many relationships, both incarnate and discarnate, how can our relationships now be our only relationships?

What you do from day to day is not necessarily all there is to your life, but the relationship that is functioning in any given moment is your relationship now. Your relationship of the moment is the only one through which you can grow now, the only one in which you can prove yourself and learn about yourself. Although much can be said about the effect that all of your relationships can have on you, the one of the moment is always the most crucial because through it you move either forward or backward.

Are you speaking of our daily casual encounters?

Any and all encounters in the course of a day are opportunities to react either constructively or deterrently to the situation at hand. Whenever you are interacting with others you are proving your mettle in the manner in which you resolve situations. No encounter is too casual to count. In fact, the way you deal with those whom you don't know personally is proof of whether you believe in the fact that we are all children of God responsible for those in need.

Every relationship is an opportunity to grow, but in order to do so you must first realize the potential inherent in every moment with another. Present-day life can be strident, rushed, aggressive. These conditions make it very difficult to understand the true nature of your contacts, even though the word contact contains an intuitive understanding of a spiritual reality.

Please explain the spiritual reality in the word contact.

We are discussing the understanding that a spiritual contact can take place in any and all encounters, casual or intimate. If you can react constructively and harmoniously to all encounters, you are indeed expressing yourself in spiritual as well as human terms, acting in accordance with God's Will for you. You have made a spiritual contact with another person, affecting that person as well as yourself constructively.

What would you say is the key to living constructively in the moment?

Honesty. Unless you are honest with yourself, your actions and reactions will be false. It is easy to confuse living comfortably with living constructively because a positive action need not necessarily be a favorable one. Honesty and courage often require a course of action you would rather not take. You are to be sufficiently concentrated on the true content of the moment in order to act in accordance with God's Will.

Of what importance is the content of the moment?

Day-by-day relationships are often dulled by the routine of living. This can best be overcome by keeping in mind not only the content of the moment, but the intent as well.

Let's say you are a discontented woman living a humdrum life, with a routine job, children who are out of hand, and a husband who takes you for granted. Nothing much seems to be happening in your life and, of course, that is the clue. You've lost sight of your intent. Was it to redeem the very relationship that now seems meaningless? Are you failing to realize that you always have a new opportunity to change, that God's Grace provides this? Perhaps the very reason you have these relationships is to develop patience, energy, courage, creativity. Perhaps the circumstances that seem boring are opportunities you need for your development.

Remember, before you can find meaning in the content of your life, you must discover its intent.

How do I do this?

You must work with the elements present in your life to create conditions of growth, just as a farmer must work with the elements presented to him. The circumstances of your life are given, just as wind, sun, earth, and rain are given to the farmer. So you must start there. You are already part of the Whole, but the Whole is not static, it fluctuates. Your relationships, like the farmer's crops, grow or wither in accordance with your ability to take responsibility for them, constantly adapting to the given circumstances that are ever changing.

What do you mean when you say the Whole fluctuates?

Circumstances alter events and events alter subsequent circumstances. This causes fluctuation in the course of events. One must go with the ebb and flow, staying with the fluctuations of the Whole and dealing with the circumstances of life as they develop throughout your sphere of influence.

Now

___

How do you see relationships in the Western world today?

There has not been time to assimilate the various elements of the scientific evolution in which our culture is involved. At first that may not seem germane to your question, but it is in fact the central reason for all the chaos that exists today. When incarnate life and free will were first granted, it was foreseen that in the progression from instinct to intuition, human beings would eventually be committed to a greater responsibility for themselves. That is what is happening today.

I see scientific advancement as the result of the development of the scientific mind. I don't see any freedom being granted, but just a natural progression of science. Please clarify this for me.

You are partially correct. However, you must understand that God's Will and God's Grace are the ever-present sources of all scientific development. The discovery of any new fact of science is in accordance with God's Will, and the opportunity to experiment a manifestation of God's Grace. These discoveries of what already exists could not be made unless free will aligned itself with God's Will. With the freedom to discover goes the responsibility for the discovery. The more complete and far-reaching the discovery, the more important responsibility becomes. Scientific advancements are intended for your benefit, not your detriment.

As God grants the opportunity for scientific discovery, He must know that irresponsibility will result. Is this as it should be?

You are overlooking the essential concern of God's Will. It is important that humans develop all possible scientific areas. Scientific discovery is merely uncovering that which already exists. The benefit that could be derived from all such discoveries far outweighs the possible deterrent results from irresponsibility. In affording the opportunity the risk is taken in the hope that the ultimate outcome will prove constructive. This becomes the responsibility of incarnates.

What is it we must do?

You need to have a clear comprehension of your role at this time so you will come to see that spiritual evolution must keep pace with mental evolution. It is not that God is abandoning you, but is allowing you greater and greater freedom to participate in the carrying out of His Will on earth. The clue to the future lies in balancing the increasing freedom to create with the responsibility for that which is created.

Is there something significant about now?

This turning point in history has accelerated in the world and in the Western world principally, because of the freedom that exists. It is especially important now, when old rules and mores around you are shifting, to remember that God's Love and God's Will are constant and that the law of cause and effect cannot be circumvented. Those who uncover or reveal God's Will as it is manifest in the physical universe work in accordance with His Will, but those who exploit it do not. This time of transition is a dangerous time because many are unable to handle the freedom involved.

What exactly do you mean?

I mean that the only way to assume responsibility for your freedom is to try always to satisfy your inner feelings stemming from your heart. Otherwise you are prone to giving in to karmic compulsion and proceeding in a deterrent way. The freedom to take advantage of scientific discoveries should not lead to rampant deterrent behavior, but that is exactly what is taking place.

What is your concept of the intention of the freedom granted in our form of government, for instance?

In conceiving of a free nation, it was never intended that freedom be separate from responsibility. But it is that which underlies all of the problems you face today.

The juxtaposition of freedom and responsibility has been fundamental to the human condition since the granting of free will. In most times and places limitations have existed, either from natural conditions such as insufficient food, or from political power. Although in the United States there are still restrictions resulting from prejudice and economics, the majority are relatively free to do what they want to do.

Now freedom has been augmented by scientific developments in the most vital areas of life — sex, procreation, and life and death themselves. Most people have not yet begun to understand the implications in this for themselves or for society. It means that the opportunity to behave responsibly has not only expanded, but has become a necessity. The greater opportunities that now exist require an understanding of the basis and continuity of life in both worlds so that wise decisions can be made.

What is the outcome of this new freedom and the temptation it produces?

The temptation of separating choice and responsibility

inevitably leads to the loss of choice. When you choose anything deterrent, whether it is drugs, power, compulsive sex, fear, violence, you diminish your freedom to choose. Irresponsibility in any area, from chemical discoveries that create the means to destroy, to new panaceas in the medicine chest to solve emotional problems, tends to leave one less free.

Those who give up their freedom in these ways move society nearer to loss of freedom for all. Emotional barriers, such as fear, envy, anger, hatred, materialize and become manifest in unsafe streets, broken homes, violent confrontations. In a society where consciousness is constantly invaded by negative forces, true freedom (inner independence) slips away almost unnoticed.

From your point of view, how does individual loss of freedom lead to loss of freedom for all?

Each individual who gives up freedom in these ways affects the freedom of all by permeating the atmosphere with negativism. As these numbers grow, so goes freedom. You are all affected by what each of you does. There is a dynamic that develops, affecting more and more people to their detriment. It takes strong defenses developed from proper preparation to withstand such negative forces.

Looking around you, you see that as areas of freedom expand, so do areas of irresponsibility, with the consequent loss of freedom itself.

V. Relationships — Unseen

Facets

It seems we've been caught up in this vortex of change so suddenly that we can't cope with it.

Not by yourselves perhaps, but remember your efforts are paralleled in the unseen world. The extremity of the present situation in the world can bring forth the energy that is needed to combat it with a paralleled response. Many in both worlds are already working to counteract deterrence and evil and allow constructive forces to assume responsibility. Many of those who work to prevent erosion of the earth or of human relationships —to prevent war, to heal, to create harmony, to bring God's Will and God's Love to others — can testify to the help they receive whether or not they realize it is a response to their own efforts. However, evil has advanced so rapidly that it will take all of your efforts and ours just to regain the balance of power.[1]

What should our efforts be to accomplish this?

You must recognize the need for construction and harmony, and act on this need. In this way you are helping not only yourself, but all of those within your sphere of influence. This is as far as one can go to alleviate the effects of deterrence and evil.

Does God have any responsibility in this?

Even though God has made it possible for humans to

---

[1] See *The Challenge of Evil* (Destiny Books, Rochester, VT, 1988).

His own responsibility. It is evident in the men and women who do His Will. This is the hope and the promise of the future. Pray that enough will be willing to abdicate self-will and give control to God before the edge of annihilation is reached.

When you say that God's responsibility is evident in those who do His Will, what exactly do you mean?

I mean that God's Will, as expressed through men and women, is proof that God remains responsible for the construction that results. All acts of construction and harmony are evidence of God's Will and God's Love and proof that God is alive and well and living in some places on earth. Our hope, as expressed in the Lord's Prayer, "Thy Kingdom come, Thy Will be done in earth as it is in Heaven," is that God will someday rule the world. But God cannot live on earth responsibly except through the alignment of humans to His Will and His Love. Where God does live on earth, construction and harmony abound.

How can we learn to see this clearly?

To get a true sense of what is happening today to human relationships I would like to help you see things as we do. Step back and, without making moral judgments, look at what is happening and consider the possibilities. Remember that anything one does creates a consequence, and that consequence creates others, and so on and on. What we would like to do is give you a sense of perspective so you can understand what is happening and arrive at the right conclusions for yourself.

I recall that you have mentioned the possibility of our spiritual selves being in more than one place at

**the same time because of needful relationships.
Just how does that work?**

The need of the spirit is to form constructive relationships. It is through them that we grow spiritually. Your
conscious self — your karmic self — is aware of only one
life at a time. However, your spiritual eternal self can
function in two or more lives at once.

Please explain how it works.

As you know, when you reincarnate your soul, your beta
body, even though invisible to you, is within you, able
to leave your body, but attached to you until death. In the
case of multiple incarnations this process is consider-
ably more advanced. Those who are developed enough
to achieve multiple incarnations function simultaneously in both the discarnate and incarnate aspects of the
world. The spiritual body functions freely even while the
incarnate body is on earth. The physical body is occu-
pied by a spirit that is able to function in both worlds
simultaneously, as well as being fully engaged in
numerous host bodies.

Just as God lives in you while you retain your own
individuality (your individuality is an element of God),
so an advanced soul's individuality can be expressed
variously.

I feel very "iffy" about this.

I suggest that you confine yourself to the concept that
great souls can and do come to earth sometimes as sev-
eral people at once in order to meet a need. Their
advancement enables them to do so.

**You have made the analogy of God within, but aren't
we also individual?**

True, but your individuality is also God. Just so, the

individuality of an advanced soul is simultaneously the individuality of the incarnate person, the discarnate soul, and an aspect of God. Remember your own beta body exists in both worlds, visiting us while you sleep. Also those who live a God-willed life are living in both worlds at once, acknowledging and communing with their discarnate loved ones daily. It is only natural then that advanced souls are capable of greater expansion and incidentally of greater accomplishment both for themselves and for others.

Why exactly would one do this?
Perhaps it is a world condition involving a great need among relationships that for constructive measures one particular soul, so segmented, may be able to accomplish most solicitously. Or maybe it is a world need requiring developed souls to return in this manner to work to alleviate the evil that has resulted from wrongdoing.

Can anyone attempt this?
No, only those who can prove their development and preparation for the task warrant such action.

What is the result of this practice?
It is a means to combat deterrence and evil.

It is what one does to alleviate a need and would not do otherwise?
It is a capability that arises in those who are advanced and prepared, when more construction than would otherwise be possible is evidently required.

And it is always connected with our relationships?
Yes, it is the need within your various relationships that triggers this action.

I expect it is impossible to grasp this process?
Yes, I'm afraid that's true.

What is the value in knowing this then?
The value to you is in seeing the importance relationships play in the function of reincarnation and the development of souls toward their goals.

I have read of great souls not only returning for world benefit, but also occupying the body of a soul to use that soul beneficially. Is this so?
Great souls are capable of doing whatever is necessary to accomplish a needed result. They not only can reincarnate and also remain in the Realms by utilizing only a segment of themselves in the incarnate world, but they could also at the same time share incarnate bodies of superior souls to help them overcome hindrances to achievement.

If great souls are motivated to return to earth by world need, are personal relationships also involved?
When you speak of world need, you are speaking of the need of individuals in the world. Great souls have multifarious relationships. They have had innumerable relationships throughout innumerable incarnations, of which large numbers are on earth at any given time. As conditions on earth negate the efforts of those toward whom the great soul feels kinship to the extent that drastic measures are called for in order to turn matters around, the decision to reincarnate is made to act as a catalyst for the constructive thrust necessary to overcome the condition.

What is the function of relationships?
The function of relationships is to grow through love.

Is concern for others an aspect of love?

Yes, it is, but we must first define just what we mean by concern. If you are implying that worry is an element here, you are mistaken. All you are doing then is making judgments about others. To have concern for the welfare of others is laudable as long as it is accomplished by tolerance and the acceptance of things as they are. The concern then results in the effort to help in any way possible without attempting to adjust conditions in accordance with a preconception of your own.

When we are faced with a problem, should we refer it to you there, should we pray about it first, or should we just take care of it in a logical manner? To what extent are we to involve your side in our daily lives?

You should always try to keep your thoughts with us. Bear in mind that the Source is here, and the solutions to all problems can be found here. What do I mean by "here"? You are to seek help from our side whenever you feel the need. I'm not saying that all of your problems are to be solved for you in this way. I am saying that you should consider your problems in the light of truth, seek help from us when necessary, and then act on your own. In this way you will be recognizing your relationship to us here and your need to learn from the Source. Decisions must always be yours, but they should come as a result of having the light of truth shed on the problems. Recognition of the need for this interaction is a growth factor to be developed.

Isn't this prayer to God?

Yes, but it is done with the knowledge that God works through people, and that all problems can have the light of truth shed upon them by someone here acting in the name of God. Through this practice a sense of relationship to discarnate souls is established. Even if you knew no one on this side, if you presented your case and listened for the answer with intensity, a thought could come to you, a flash, revealing truth that could be beneficial.

Isn't this communication?

Not really because there is no extended conversation with a particular soul. Rather the answer comes as hunches, definitive words, a rush of thought, a clear picture, to those who are alerted to the moment. Attention to the moment is essential, and even then it takes many trials to get in the groove. Perseverance is the answer to success in this venture.

Why not just bring our problems to God?

When you do this, your problems are being considered by servants and messengers of God. The purpose is for you to develop a relationship with those of us here who serve God in this way. Many, many souls who have access to truth to help solve all human problems attend God in this manner.

When you tell us to be so concentrated on doing God's Will that we will become conduits, how is this accomplished? What should we keep in mind?

Try always to hold the realization that all thought, all conversation, and all acts can occur in our presence, but only as you give permission through awareness. You are to increase your awareness to include us at all times.

What is the need?

The need is for understanding. If you know you have our ear whenever you want it, you can then consider events as they are taking place with us. Your desire will be to include us in all events, in all decision-making, and in all problems as they occur.

Do you mean that our first reaction should be to turn to you there?

Yes, exactly. Here is where you will learn to see things as they are. Remember, God works through people, perfect souls capable of serving God as messengers. Among such souls will be relationships of yours.

Is it possible to be related to such beings?

Relationship is always present in your lives. If you live alone, if you are reclusive, you still have relationships that affect you in your day-to-day living. If you are without an incarnate family you still have a discarnate family, some members of which are ready and willing to help when called upon.

But wouldn't this require belief in their existence?

Most people have at least a vague belief in an afterlife and the value of prayer. By praying for your discarnate loved ones and asking them to pray for you, you are opening a channel through which the Law of Parallels and reciprocity can function. Those discarnate relationships who are able will certainly respond to your hopes and desires as well as your problems and needs. At your instigation, benefit can result.

God's Kingdom

You have spoken of God's Kingdom. Please explain just what that is.

Your question exemplifies the fact that even though people may have a profound belief in God, and even may have experienced His Reality, their belief in the actuality of His Kingdom is exceedingly vague. God does exist in the unseen for most people, but the rest of the unseen is either stereotyped as heaven or hell or has no existence at all.

The ancient sense of intimacy with the unseen has been banished by modern technology, and God's Kingdom has been reduced by many who do believe to a place of "eternal rest" with angels, but no living human souls.

The unseen is no longer a pleasant place, or even a fearsome place. It is not much of anything — a place of nonactivity, of nothingness. However, although science has put constraints on your imagination and intuition, there is evidence that imagination and intuition are nevertheless beginning to lead science itself to the unseen.

In addition, life after physical death is achieving a much more graphic kind of reality through the work of those who report and record afterlife and out-of-body experiences.

The Unobstructed Universe *by Stewart Edward White made the discarnate world real to us, with the realization that this is indeed one world, that we*

occupy the same space only on different frequencies.
Please take us further with this.

In addition to the understanding that the Whites were able to convey of time, space, and motion, I would like to give you a clearer understanding of one aspect of this — place. Place as we experience it here is where we are in our own development. The concepts I have given you of the Realms, the Place of Preparation, the Place of Self-Deception, and the Lower Regions[1] are where souls truly are. This is determined by frequency, which fluctuates in accordance with spiritual development.

You too live in this way psychologically. Your spiritual frequency is determined by everything that you really are, and that, in turn, determines where you are psychologically. You recognize this in common speech. When you say things such as "I can't imagine where his head is," or "I know where you're coming from," or "he is a close friend," you are describing a psychological place.

It sounds as though you are in a constant state of
flux. Is there anything stable?

Stability and change are simultaneous here just as they are for you. Think how your physical relationships change. First you relate to others as an infant, then as a child, then as a teenager, a maturing adult, and so forth, until old age. Nevertheless you are the same person through these changes.

Those who have come to our aspect of the world ahead of you have simply taken another step. By relating to them, you reinforce your belief in the continuity of life

---

[1] See *The Challenge of Evil* (Destiny Books, Rochester, VT, 1988).

and so alleviate your own fear of death. Belief in reincarnation allows you to identify an individual as one
whose life has gone on rather than one whose life has
ended. Take our relationship, for instance. For a while
I was Richard who was your close friend. Then I was
Richard who had been killed. Now I am Richard who
works with you. In all of these aspects I have remained
the same essential person, subject to spiritual development. This is important to grasp because it helps you to
see your own life more clearly.

Do your relationships change in a similar manner in the unseen world?

It is expressed differently. Rather than an outward physical change that conditions the inward changes, it is the
opposite. The inner state of one's being affects the outward change. Aura and color, for instance, are the consequence of inner conditions. Relationships, therefore,
do not differ because you have changed in the sense of
growing older (you always appear in the prime of life),
but because of spiritual changes. This rearranges and
changes relationships.

Is there any way to prepare ourselves for this?

If you think of your present relationships in this way it
will help you when you reach the unseen world to accept
the relationships as they are then and there. Not only will
you see yourself and others as they are, but you will come
to understand what that means to you. You will understand better what karmic burdens you have been carrying for a long time, and you will also become aware of
those you have most recently accumulated, and how
they have affected your relationships.

Isn't there a danger that preoccupation with the dead can become morbid?

But of course they are *not* dead. They are very much alive. If your concern becomes morbid, it is not honest. Reaching out to those in the unseen world should become an adventure. Those who ignore their "dead" are apt to become fearful of death. Those who express a continuing positive interest in and concern for their loved ones who have experienced physical death are acknowledging their belief in life. I am not, of course, referring to the dead body, but to the living spirit.

All expressions of reverence, from primitive ceremonies to a great requiem mass, are acts of love. On the other hand, not only the denial of death but even efforts to deny the natural aging process become a self-perpetrating form of fear. Sudden death is difficult because it robs the person of the opportunity to approach the transition gradually, allowing time for the adjustment.

How should we relate to all of our loved ones who have gone on?

When I speak about relating to those who are here, I am not talking about communication. Communication, if you remember, is a talent that some people may develop. But the ability to relate to those of us in this aspect of reality is a matter of heart. Pray for us. Pray for us as we pray for you.

Grieving only holds the one you love back. You should rejoice that a new phase of the journey has begun.

Should we think this way even if the death has come with the person unrepentant?

Under such conditions your job would be even more

important. You must hold positive thoughts. You must know that the person will be helped, not only by your prayers but also by souls on the other side. You must believe in whatever you found good in that person and know that your belief in itself will be helpful.

We know that we have incarnate families. Do families exist in the discarnate world too?
All of the relationships you have on earth are important. They contribute to your development. But by the very nature of the function of reincarnation, they vary each time and are often transitory. The only relationships of lasting value are your spiritual family. This family evolves. Simply defined, it is those with whom you have had a close family relationship through many incarnations on earth and with whom you share the same final goal. This spiritual family exists in potential throughout your cycle of reincarnations, both on earth and in the Place of Preparation. It becomes actual as you reach out intuitively and develop these relationships constructively. But it is not until the Realms have been reached that the spiritual family becomes aware of its own true reality.

You have said that once we reach the Realms we are on our own except for encouragement and love from others there.[1] Does this constitute a family?
Your ultimate goal is to become an integral element of an order of the evolving Body of God. Your spiritual family, then, includes all the other elements (souls) of your ultimate goal. In the Realms, the other members

---

[1] See The Realms, *The Challenge of Evil* (Destiny Books, Rochester, VT, 1988).

of your family who are more developed encourage you, express their love, and try in every way to help you keep your eyes on the pinnacle. You do the same for those less developed than you. Family denotes a bonding with God the Father–Mother.

The Fellowships

Are there any relationships that are peculiar to the discarnate world?
The Fellowships in the Place of Preparation fit that category.

How are they organized?
By goals.

Is there a Fellowship for every goal?
Yes.

Why are they called Fellowships?
There is no perfect word in English that expresses the particular sense of mystical bonding. Fellowship does convey the idea of purposeful bonding through friendship or comradeship without personal involvement.

What is the purpose of the Fellowships?
To advance toward a goal through understanding and growth in relationships, thereby preparing to overcome deterrence and evil wherever possible.

Why the need?
Because the ultimate state will be the ultimate condition of Fellowship realized. Fellowships foster oneness in shared pursuit, shared knowledge, and comprehension that leads to spiritual growth. A common bond through goals is shared with others and with the

Father–Mother. All living things are related to each other and to the Father–Mother. Some are close and some are distant, but all are related to God. We are all one in God. Remember, each Fellowship will ultimately become a distinct organ in the augmented Body of God, each member contributing an individual, unique, and perfect element of that organ without which it would be incomplete.

All incarnates long intuitively for the ecstatic state of oneness which is to be our ultimate reward, but many of them don't know what growth that end requires. In seeking it they too often resort to other means to create instant euphoria, however fleeting, through the use of alcohol, drugs, sex, etc. But since this pursuit never truly satisfies the longing, not knowing what else to do in the absence of self-knowledge, they are at the mercy of their unfulfilled aberrations.

Do all those of the same goal join their Fellowships?

Most do, but some who are not seeing this clearly enough to recognize its value prefer to create their own environment within which to function. However, as they develop more understanding they invariably become affiliated with the Fellowship of their final goal.

Do you mean that all the while souls are preparing to reincarnate they automatically belong to the Fellowship of their specific goal?

No, that's not it. Those who belong are those who choose to partake of specific extracurricular activities that relate to ultimate purpose. They espouse the common cause of their specific goal and they develop the relationships that can help in their present efforts to move on. The Fellowships bolster individual effort so they can leave properly prepared for their next immediate incarnate experience.

Do they have leaders?
The leaders of the Fellowships come from the First Realm.

Do the Fellowships have any other function than that of promoting self-knowledge?
They form the various segments that comprise the Forces of Light. A great deal of effort goes into contacting those of their ultimate goal in the incarnate world in an effort to bring them to clearer vision about intent, purpose, and the necessity for construction (understanding the necessity of following God's Will). Working as a unit they bring greater strength to their efforts in calling on Constructive Force to augment them.

Just how does this function?
It functions as a guard armed with construction and made up of five units determined by goal. Each unit utilizes whatever elements of its particular purpose are available to it, with love permeating the entire effort. Their efforts are to induce uncommitted incarnates to resist the grasp of the Forces of Darkness by deflecting their compulsive karma toward constructive thought, thereby lessening the power of evil and promoting construction and harmony.

Does everyone in the Place of Preparation want to belong?
No one is forced to join, although all are eligible.

Why wouldn't one want to join?
Those who think that any distraction that diverts attention from basics is confusing do not readily join the Fellowships. However, as development of needed qualities takes place, they come to see the advantages of sharing

and learning from their relationships there. They then find the companionship and purpose most beneficial.

How and why did the Fellowships form?
The need for Fellowships developed soon after the function of reincarnation started. From the beginning...

In the middle of this sentence I got a flash that they were part of the structure of reincarnation as God conceived it. Am I correct?
...yes, as God conceived it Fellowships were to be made up of all those who had experienced relationships of varying kinds with each other — as husband, wife, sister, brother, father, mother, cousin, friend, lover, etc., over and over, switching sexes and roles in the process and continuing for as long as necessary. In the Place of Preparation they became members of the same Fellowship. Their relationships are furthered in this way, and through what is gained they finally make their decision about parents each time.

Do true relationships always mean those of the same ultimate goal?
Yes.

Do you mean we have no real relationships with those of different goals?
You have no profound relationships with them.

What about casual relationships?
Casual is on the periphery of relationships. Acquaintanceship is more the word for it. Acquaintanceship is not a meaningful relationship. You may be bound by blood, but if you are not also bound by goal even a blood relationship can be casual. A casual friendly acquaintanceship with those of different goals is common.

Is it possible that various lifetimes of relationships could be present at one time in a Fellowship?

Oh yes. If you consider the average lifetime on earth and compare this to the length of time (your time) the average soul stays in the Place of Preparation (from a few months to thousands of years your time) you can see how easy it could be to trace your relationships back through endless incarnations gaining understanding in the process.

What brings about the extreme difference in length of stay there?

In the spirit of fellowship the need for solidifying various relationships and mending the tears in others is apparent. Through the understanding gained by the teaching within the Fellowship itself, along with the acquisition of needed qualities for reincarnating, a soul feels the need to remain in the Place of Preparation for a protracted period of time.

On the other hand, there are those who feel an overwhelming desire to continue a relationship that existed at death in the incarnate world, so they decide to return within the immediate family with whom they are still involved. Such a need could cause one to reincarnate as soon as a host (embryo) becomes available in the family. This could be a matter of a few years or even months. This explains the great diversity in time spent in the Place of Preparation.

Would you say that all who reincarnate early come ill-prepared?

This is true of most of them. Their concern for being with others robs them of understanding the need for their own development. They tend to believe that the incarnate relationship for which they long will help them. This could be true to some extent if the relationship they seek is constructive, but nothing can take the place of time spent in the Place of Preparation. However, the magnetic power of relationships cannot be underestimated.

What is meant by "in the spirit of fellowship"?

It is the atmosphere created within a particular Fellowship. All who belong know their particular ultimate goal, and they learn what elements are still needed to achieve its realization. They see where they are to go and just how far they have come. They recognize the need for certain attitudes of mind, and the atmosphere generated within the Fellowship facilitates this understanding to a great extent. The spirit of a particular Fellowship permeates all, encouraging harmony, aspiration, and oneness.

Why are Fellowships necessary?

Fellowships are the life blood of final goals. They furnish the elements that will be put to use when fully perfected in the ultimate augmented evolving Body of God. Through the efforts of the Fellowships cohesion develops, and each time a soul returns to the Place of Preparation the work that will result in perfect cohesion of function is taken up again with further accomplishment.

Developed souls in all of the various Fellowships contribute the best they have to give to mankind as their own growth factors. All possible constructive avenues are explored and made effective through the efforts of those who live in true fellowship.

The Ultimate Relationship

How would you define God's relationship to us?

"Behold, I stand at the door and knock. If any man hear my voice and open the door, I will come in to him and will sup with him, and he with me."[1]

God's relationship with us is in the active voice. God is not sitting quietly in His Kingdom waiting for us to come to Him. On the contrary. See what happens when you reduce this passage to the verbs: Behold — stand —knock — hear — open — will come in — sup.

Here is the movement, the urge, the yearning of God to reach you, to be heard by you, to be welcomed, to stand by you and share with you. All you are asked to do is open the door and listen.

You can learn about this by arresting the moment. Stop whatever you are doing and ask, "Is God with me? Do I recognize God's presence? Am I listening? Is our relationship now in action? Am I an open conduit for God's Love and God's Will, or have I shut God out for the time being?" You will discover there is no such thing as a nonrelationship. A seeming nonrelationship is a negative relationship. You are either for God or against God.

"Behold, I stand at the door and knock." This marvelous statement is very potent in itself, but how do we open the door and to whom exactly? You have said that God works through others, but if we put

---

[1] Rev. 3:20.

Jesus at the door, what about all those who believe in other revealers? Could it be that it is God in each of us that is knocking?

You are all wound up, but you have given the subject thought. Let me clarify immediately. The One who is knocking at your door is the One closest to you — God in you. God in you wants to enter your daily life and be the motivating element of your being. Your spirit (God) has come with you in the hope that you will recognize the importance of living together, shedding your faults, and gaining qualities that will bring you closer to your goal.

How am I able to hear God knocking?

God is life. God is love. With every beat of your heart you are made aware of the presence of God reminding you to live by your heart feelings and allow them (God) to reclaim your life. Through your heart you express love, aligning yourself with God in you and bringing God to earth. By consulting your sense of truth, by loving and trusting your intuition, you are utilizing your spiritual equipment, and the Will of God in you becomes your will.

How does the arrested moment relate to the eternal now?

Actually the arrested moment is another way of thinking of the eternal now. Ideally the kind of awareness achieved in the arrested moment becomes constant, becomes your life lived in awareness of the presence of God. To even approach that requires constant involvement in bringing yourself back to awareness, and then holding that awareness in your heart while living your ordinary day-to-day life.

As it is, most people live days, weeks, years, and even most of their lives scarcely conscious of God at all, and those who are may often define it in different terms.

Intuitive belief in the essential goodness of life, in the power of spirit, serves many better than rigidly held beliefs that can cut off all intuition. Whatever your mode of thought is, it is through your spiritual equipment that you know God, that you can recognize the benevolence and healing power of Constructive Force, achieving oneness with God.

You've said that oneness with God is a paradox, but I'm not sure I remember why.

The more truly we are one with God, the more we become one with all. The more we become one with all, the more we are individual. The more we relinquish control of our lives to God, the more we are free.

When you say "to become one with God," are you referring to God in us?

Yes, your higher self-God-ruling your life.

Just how does being one with all make us more individual?

Through love you relate to others and reveal yourself as God-centered, from which your individuality shines forth, developing as you continue to love others.

How does relinquishing control make us free?

By eliminating self you are allowing God to rule, relieving you of self-imposed responsibility.

What about those who don't relate to God at all?

There is really no such thing as a nonrelationship with God. One who ignores God or never thinks about God is in just as real a relationship as one who is filled with faith. The importance of a relationship with God is equal for all whether you know it or not; it is a living reality.

It changes with every thought, every act, every breath you take. You are constantly going with it or withdrawing from it. It is never passive.

You say that those who never think of God have just as real a relationship as those who are filled with faith. How do you explain this?

Whether or not you acknowledge it, your relationship to God does exist. Even if you choose to ignore God, God isn't ignoring you, and in times of need or dire stress, you may very well find yourself seeking God's comfort and guidance, calling for help in spite of yourself. How much better to be with God, to relate to God in you and become obedient to that higher self. In this way you are not in conflict with God's Will, you become one with God's Will, utilizing your spiritual equipment to raise your frequency.

It's hard to believe in a relationship with God since it seems so one-sided.

From God's side it must indeed seem one-sided, since a conscious relationship of even devoted souls with God is at best sporadic, with periods of doubt and confusion intervening. Generally it is felt only under stress. However, when such encounters do occur, they can become so profound that they affect the rest of a life beneficially.

What is the nature of such encounters? What happens?

Try to understand this: When your need is great everything else diminishes in importance, and all of your energy becomes concentrated on your need. This energy combined with the need opens up an avenue of belief that, in itself, leads you to the presence of God. So we have the elements of concentration, energy, and need. But because God is invisible, you must add another — faith. Faith is reinforced by belief, and belief, in turn, is reinforced by experience. As you live in faith you experience God in your life. This sometimes manifests itself in startling ways, but more often in subtle patterns —things happen to you that are right, or that you come to see are right — a pattern forms — your life takes shape — you proceed.

Don't I myself take part in this?

Put self aside and listen. Accept your incarnate self as the means through which your discarnate self (God in you) can achieve oneness. Oneness is not an intellectual concept, but a reality. Your love for God must be expressed through you in love for others. In this way you are acknowledging and achieving oneness with God.

What is the reality of the ultimate relationship?

You need God, but God also needs you. Belief in yourself as a functioning part of the Whole strengthens your belief that the relationship God has made possible is to serve Him as coworker on earth. You are the reality of God on earth when you love one another as God loves you. All of your relationships become a means toward this end.

Other books by Graham Bernard

Why You Are Who You Are
A Psychic Conversation

When Graham Bernard first began his explorations into
psychic communication, little did he expect the remarkable
encounter that awaited him. A relationship, interrupted two
decades earlier by the untimely death of his friend, Richard,
was instantly renewed.
Gradually Richard became the author's inspiration for a
lifetime of dedicated spiritual work.

This first book in the series of channeled teachings of Richard
reveals the significance of our earthly experiences and offers
an understanding of life's most perplexing issues, including
immortality, reincarnation, the purpose of human existence,
individual destinies, and the role of thought and attitude in
determining our life's course.

ISBN 0-89281-100-5
$8.95 paperback

The Challenge of Evil
Further Conversations with Richard
Graham Bernard

Channeling the teachings of his spirit guide, Richard, Graham Bernard probes into one of the most complex puzzles of human experience: the meaning of evil and the purpose of our struggle with the dark side of human nature.

As introduced in his first book, Why You Are Who You Are, the concepts of "construction" and "deterrence" are shown to be the positive and negative forces with which we constantly contend. The Challenge of Evil explores deterrence in detail, focusing on the responsibility of each human being to choose between good and evil. It clarifies subjects such as the origin of deterrent force, the meaning and function of relationships, self-judgment, individuality, karma, and faith.

ISBN 0-89281-205-2
$8.95 paperback

"Clear, straightforward, concerned with all aspects of life, death, and rebirth." —The Book Reader

How to Read the Aura, Practice Psychometry, Telepathy, and Clairvoyance
W.E. Butler

A renowned British parapsychologist shows how to develop the higher faculties of consciousness as he explains the four psychic powers that reside within each of us:

• Perceive and understand the meaning of the energy field that surrounds all living creatures

• Read the psychic emanations emitted by all objects

• Communicate thoughts through the power of mind

• See the future, the past, and the unlimited present

ISBN 0-89281-161-7
$6.95 paperback

"Easily draws the skeptic into the realm of belief."
— The Psychic Reader

Centering
A Guide to Inner Growth
Sanders G. Laurie and Melvin J. Tucker

If you want to get more out of life, have better health and
relief from stress, this system of meditation offers a unique
key to personal fulfillment. Starting with a simple
psychological test that helps you identify the way in which
you perceive the world, you will learn how to build upon this
understanding to increase your learning power, enhance and
utilize your talents, build up your psychic energies and
defenses, transmit healing, and interpret the symbolism of
dreams. This book will enable you to attain, at your own
pace, the self-realization and well-being you seek.

ISBN 0-89281-050-5
$6.95 paperback

These and other Inner Traditions titles are available at many
fine bookstores or, to order direct, send a check or money
order, plus $2.00 shipping and handling for the first book and
$1.00 for each additional book, to:

Inner Traditions
One Park Street
Rochester, VT 05767

A complete catalog of books from Inner Traditions is available
upon request from the above address.